THE JESUS FILES

Written and Designed by
Doug Powell

THE LIFE OF OUR LORD AND SAVIOUR JESUS CHRIST.

The Jesus Files
Published by B&H Publishing Group
One LifeWay Plaza
Nashville, TN 37234

©2014 Doug Powell
Written and designed by Doug Powell

First Printing: May 2014
Printed by Lake Book Manufacturing
ISBN: 9780805499292
All scripture quotations are from
The Holman Christian Standard Bible

More has been written about Jesus Christ than any other person who ever lived. But how much can we really know about Jesus?

The Jesus Files takes you on a tour of his life. Using paintings and vintage photos of the Holy Land, The Jesus Files captures the reality of the events, places, and people in the life of Christ. Plus, the meaning of Jesus and the theological importance of the events of his life are explained as you explore the greatest story ever told—or shown!

Then, dig in and investigate the historical evidence for the resurrection of Jesus Christ. Learn the facts the vast majority of scholars agree on and how the Resurrection is the only explanation that makes sense of them all. Get equipped to give an answer to anyone who asks why they should believe in Jesus Christ.

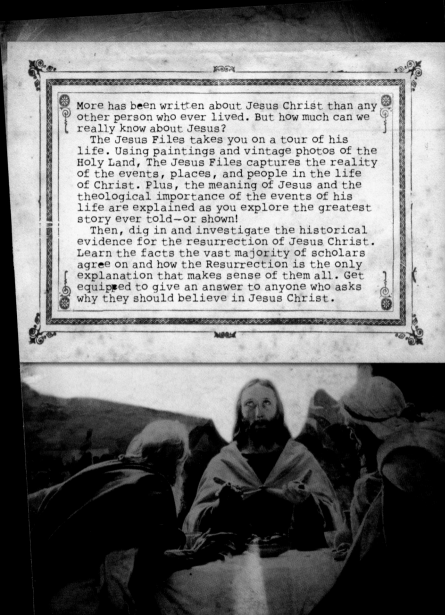

Annunciation

Mary was probably a young teenager when the angel Gabriel appeared to her and told her she would have a son even though she was a virgin. He also said her son would be the promised Messiah. Lastly, he told her that Elizabeth, her relative, was six months pregnant even though she was old and was not able to conceive until now. This put Mary in a tough spot since she was engaged to be married to Joseph. If it was discovered that she was pregnant then people in Nazareth would assume she had been unfaithful to Joseph, and adultery was a sin punishable by death. So Mary left Nazareth and went to the hill country of Judea to visit Elizabeth.

The Virgin's Well in Nazareth.

Hebron in the hill country of Judea

After being given the startling revelation that she would give birth to a child that was the long-awaited Messiah, Mary may have questioned whether she understood the vision correctly. We don't know what was going through her mind, but if we put ourselves in her place it's easy to see how she may have been confused or scared. But when she arrived at Elizabeth's house she received confirmation immediately. Elizabeth's baby, who would become known as John the Baptist, leapt in her womb, and she declared Mary's baby would be her Lord. This must have given Mary great relief and confidence since she responded with a hymn of praise that showed she understood, at least in part, the great gift that her son would be to the world.

Nazareth Street Scene

When Mary returned to Nazareth after staying in Judea for three months, her pregnancy would have begun to show. She knew that by returning to Nazareth she faced rumours, ridicule, condemnation, and even a possible death penalty. But she trusted God to be faithful and to provide for her.

When Joseph learned Mary was pregnant he decided to quitely divorce her and protect her from as much humiliation as he could. But an angel appeared to Joseph and told him to go through with the wedding. The angel also told Joseph that Mary had conceived through the Holy Spirit and that their son would save his people from their sins. Mary may have told Joseph about her vision, but it must have sounded like a story she made up to hide the shame of adultery. But now Joseph was told the same thing. For the next six months they must have wondered just what this special baby would be like when he was born.

Nazareth

The Virgin's Well in Nazareth.

THEOLOGICAL IMPORTANCE

The Annunciation of Jesus' incarnation to Mary is the fulfillment of the prophecy that God would send a Messiah to save his people. It is also the fulfillent of the prophecy in Isaiah 7:14 that the Messiah would be born of a virgin.

While Mary was still pregnant, Caesar Augustus took a census. Jews preferred to be counted in their hometown. So Joseph took Mary and went to where his family was from—Bethlehem. This fulfilled the prophecy in Micah 5:2 that the Messiah would be from Bethlehem.

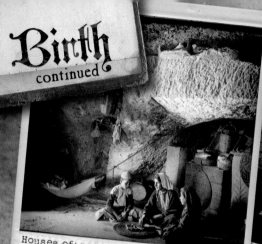

Houses often were built over or inside caves. There were many homes like this in Bethlehem. This is probably the kind of home Jesus was born in.

A common three room house in Israel. The "inn" or "upper room" is here:

After 9 months of knowing the baby she was carrying was the promised Messiah, Mary may have been surprised by how ordinary her labor and delivery was, as well as the appearance of her baby. She may have even questioned whether she had understood the angel's message correctly. But as she held her newborn baby, she received confirmation because the shepherds arrived to worship the baby.

Shepherds in the fields of Bethlehem

Joseph and Mary went to Bethlehem because it was Joseph's hometown. That means he probably had relatives there, and therefore the first place he would go would be to their house. The typical house in Israel had three rooms. One for cooking and sleeping, one for the animals, and one for guests. The guest room gets translated as "inn" in our English Bibles. We think of an inn as a hotel, and the Greek word can mean that. But Bethlehem was too small to have a hotel and

it was not on a major road where a hotel would be needed. Many guest rooms were above the rest of the house and were called upper rooms." Luke uses the same Greek word to refer to the upper room where the Last Supper took place and the "inn" that was full in Bethlehem. But when Luke records the parable of the Good Samaritan he uses the Greek word that can only mean "hotel." He may have used a different word to record Jesus' birth because it was not a hotel.

THEOLOGICAL IMPORTANCE

The birth of Jesus is the arrival of the Savior of the world. Ironically, it indicates the condemnation of humanity by saying we are utterly lost, need rescuing, and cannot save ourselves. But it's also the source of our only hope of salvation.

This also explains why the inn (the guest room) was full. Joseph probably had other relatives that had to return to Bethlehem for the census and had arrived earlier than he and Mary did. And these other relatives were given the guest room. So Joseph and Mary stayed in the only room left, the one for the animals.

Birth

Jesus was probably not born on December 25th. In fact, the earliest Christians did not celebrate Jesus' birth, only his Resurrection. It wasn't until the end of the fourth century that the church started celebrating Christmas. Even then there were at least three different days that were used. The date they eventually settled on was the date of the popular pagan festival of Saturnalia. They kept the time of the holiday but changed what was being celebrated.

In the 5th century a monk named Dionysius who was trained in astronomy and mathematics made a calendar based on the birth of Jesus. He calculated the time between the founding of Rome and the birth of Jesus to be 753 years. Later it was discovered that Herod died 749 years after the founding of Rome, making our calendar at least 4 years and maybe up to 7 years off. So Jesus was born between 4-7 BC.

Bethlehem is about eighty-five miles south of Nazareth. Jews from Galilee often went around Samaria because Samaritans were considered unclean and heretical. Since Mary could probably travel only about ten miles a day in her condition, it would have taken over a week to get to Bethlehem.

Background: The Church of the Nativity in Bethlehem.

In the second century the emperor Hadrian tried to destroy all Christian holy sites. In Jerusalem, he leveled Golgotha, filled in the tomb with dirt, and built a pagan temple on top of it. In Bethlehem, he filled in the cave where Jesus was born and planted a grove of trees on top of it.

Traditional birth spot

In both cases Hadrian marked these spots instead of destroying them. When Constantine's mother Helena toured the Holy Land in the early 4th century, she ordered these sites be restored. The Church of the Nativity was built on top of the cave home traditionally thought to be the birth place of Jesus.

Traditional spot of the manger

When the magi arrived from the east they may have found a toddler Jesus, not a newborn baby. Matthew and Luke use the Greek words for both newborn and small child at different parts in their Gospels. The Magi had followed a star which stopped over the place where Jesus was. Because a star in the sky cannot pinpoint a specific house, the star was most likely a miraculous event and not an astronomical event. There may have been an astronomical event at the time but the magi could not have found Jesus using only that

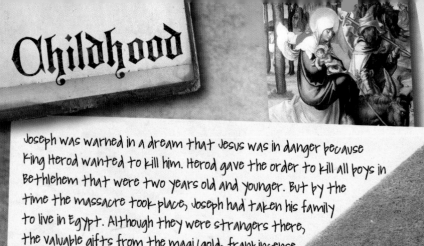

Childhood

Joseph was warned in a dream that Jesus was in danger because King Herod wanted to kill him. Herod gave the order to kill all boys in Bethlehem that were two years old and younger. But by the time the massacre took place, Joseph had taken his family to live in Egypt. Although they were strangers there, the valuable gifts from the magi (gold, frankincense, and myrrh) were able to be used to buy and trade for all their needs while in Egypt. Their escape to Egypt allowed the prophecy of Hosea 11:1 to be fulfilled— "Out of Egypt I called My son."

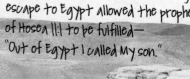

Road with Nazareth in the background

Jesus' childhood is important because it shows that he was fully human in every way. He grew, learned, had family, learned a trade, and worshipped just as everyone else did and just as we do today. Jesus' childhood reinforces the fully human nature that is necessary for him to be a proper mediator between God and Man.

Eventually, Joseph received another visitation from an angel in a dream telling him that Herod had died and that he should return to Israel. At first, Joseph thought about returning to Bethlehem, which may mean the family had moved there permanently before escaping to Egypt. But when he learned that Herod's son was the new ruler there he decided to take the family to Mary's hometown of Nazareth. Matthew writes that this fulfilled the prophecy that the messiah would be called a Nazarene (Matt. 2:23).

Background: Nazareth

Childhood

continued

Nazareth probably had about 1,800 people at the time Jesus grew up there. His family was very typical. He had at least four half-brothers (James, Joses, Judas, and Simon) and at least two half-sisters (whose names we do not know).

Later, when Jesus started his ministry, his siblings not only rejected his teachings, they thought he was insane. In fact, most people in Nazareth rejected Jesus. But after Jesus' death, James and Judas became convinced Jesus was who he claimed to be—the Son of God, Messiah. James even became the leader of the church in Jerusalem and was martyred for believing Jesus—his own brother—was God incarnate.

Jesus learned the trade of his father. Although the English translation is "carpenter," the original Greek word for Jesus' trade can also mean "builder," or "craftsman" like a stone mason. It was the hard manual labor of a peasant. This might be why Luke 2:40 describes Jesus as "strong" as well as filled with wisdom. He was also well liked by the people he lived among according to Luke 2:52.

Jesus probably knew three languages: Hebrew, Aramaic, and Greek, which was the common language of the day.

A carpenter in Nazareth

WE KNOW VERY LITTLE ABOUT JESUS' CHILDHOOD. EXCEPT FOR HIS BIRTH AND ESCAPE TO EGYPT, THE ONLY STORY WE HAVE IS FROM WHEN JESUS WAS 12. HIS FAMILY HAD TRAVELLED TO JERUSALEM TO CELEBRATE PASSOVER, BUT AS THEY WERE RETURNING HOME THEY REALIZED HE WAS NOT WITH THEM (THEIR FAMILY WAS TRAVELLING WITH A NUMBER OF OTHER FAMILIES). JOSEPH AND MARY RETURNED TO JERUSALEM AND FOUND HIM IN THE TEMPLE LEARNING FROM THE TEACHERS THERE. JESUS ASKED HIS PARENTS WHY THEY HAD BEEN SEARCHING FOR HIM—DIDN'T THEY KNOW HE WOULD BE IN HIS FATHER'S HOUSE? HIS QUESTION SHOWS THAT HE HAD AN AWARENESS OF WHO HE WAS AT AN EARLY AGE.

ALTHOUGH THERE ARE BOOKS THAT CLAIM TO RECORD JESUS' CHILDHOOD, THEY HAVE BEEN REJECTED FROM INCLUSION IN THE BIBLE FOR MANY REASONS. ONE IS THAT THEY WERE ALL WRITTEN AFTER THE LAST APOSTLE DIED. ANOTHER IS THAT THE TEACHINGS IN THE BOOKS DIRECTLY CONTRADICT THE KNOWN TEACHINGS OF JESUS. MOST OF THESE BOOKS WERE WRITTEN BY MEMBERS OF HERETICAL SECTS THAT WERE TRYING TO MAKE JESUS OUT TO BE ONE OF THEM INSTEAD OF LETTING JESUS' TEACHINGS STAND ON THEIR OWN.

Baptism

Traditional spot of Jesus' baptism.

The first event in the New Testament is not the annunciation to Mary but the appearance of the angel Gabriel to her relative Zechariah. Gabriel told him that he would have a son who would prepare the way for the coming of the Lord. In other words, John would be the last prophet of the Old Testament era. He would proclaim the coming of the messiah. John's message included preaching a baptism for the forgiveness of sins. As a result, he became known as "John the Baptizer" or "John the Baptist."

John's baptism did not take away the sins of anyone. His baptism was a ceremonial cleansing that happened after a person had repented of their sins and committed themselves to follow God's law. In fact, at that time baptism was the final stage in how a Gentile became a Jew. John baptized both Gentile and Jew because by doing so they were declaring themselves to be part of the faithful remnant of Israel—the true believers rather than people who believed they were saved just by being Jewish.

When Jesus came to John to be baptized, John didn't want to do it. After all, Jesus had no sins to repent of and therefore did not need to be ceremonially cleansed. But Jesus insisted that John do it. The baptism did not cleanse him from sin, but declared him clean from sin. And by being baptized he was identifying with those in the past who believed in the promise of his coming and those who would believe that he had come.

After Jesus came up out of the water a voice was heard from heaven that said, "This is My beloved Son. I take delight in Him!" And the Holy Spirit descended on him with the appearance of a dove. This is the clearest example in scripture of the three members of the Trinity.

THEOLOGICAL IMPORTANCE

Jesus said his baptism was necessary to fulfill all righteousness. Although he didn't need to repent from sin or be cleansed, he used his baptism to be declared clean from sin. And in being baptized he was identifying with those who would follow him.

Temptation

Immediately after his baptism Jesus was led by the Holy Spirit into the Judean wilderness for 40 days. While he was there he was tempted by Satan. Adam and Eve were tempted in a garden where everything was perfect and all their needs were provided for. And yet they failed to keep God's law. Jesus was tempted in a fallen world, a wilderness where he had none of his needs met. And yet he succeeded in keeping God's law by clinging to God's word. In many ways this event was set in the opposite conditions of Satan's temptation of Adam and Eve.

Temptation

"If you are the Son of God, throw yourself down from here..."

sin: unbelief

Response: "Do not test the Lord your God." (Deut 6:16)

Satan urges Jesus to test God's word, to not believe just because God said it. again, this is what satan did with adam and Eve at the fall (you shall not surely die!). Jesus understands that putting God to the test requires god to live up to human standards, which is a reversal of the way God made the world.

Temptation

"To you I will give all this authority and their glory, for it has been delivered to me, and I give it to whom I will. If you, then, will worship me, it will all be yours."

sin: pride

response: "Worship the Lord your God and serve only him." (Deut 6:13)

Satan offers Jesus a way to establish a kingdom over all the world without having to go to the cross. He appeals to Jesus' human pride. But Jesus understood the kingdom he came to rule required victory over sin And required obedience to the Father. If Jesus had fallen for this temptation then even though he might rule, he would not be worthy of worship.

Temptation

""If you are the Son of God, command this stone to become bread."

sin: greed

Response: "Man must not live on bread alone, but on every word that comes from the mouth of God." (Deut 8:3)

Satan tries to convince jesus that God has not fulfilled all of Jesus' needs. This is the same approach Satan used with Eve in Genesis 3. but Jesus is satisfied through obedience to the father, not through earthly indulgences. And by responding with scripture, Jesus teaches that knowing the word is not enough; the word must be obeyed.

Background: Mount of Temptation

Ministry

Most of Jesus' ministry was focused in Galilee, especially the early and middle phases of his work. Toward the end of his ministry he began to focus on Judea much more. This was part of what brought him into conflict with the Jewish leadership and eventually led to his crucifixion.

Fishermen on the Sea of Galilee

Sidon

Bron van de Jordaan

Ennon

Tyrus

't Water van Merom

Capernaum

GALILEE

De Galileesche Zee

Ptolemais Nazareth

de Beek Kison

OOST

de Berg Carmel

de Beek Jabok

Cezarea

SAMARIA

Jordaan Riv.

Samaria

de Beek Jazer

Joppe

ERFDEEL van den Vorst van ISRAËL

PEREA

Akkaron

de Beek Arnon

Jerusalem

't MEIR van

Gaza JUDEA

SODOM of

DOODE ZEE

Beek Bezor

Background: Samaria

Women were very important to Jesus' ministry, and at least several women were part of the group that travelled with him. Jesus' ministry, like all ministries, needed money to feed and provide for those who were a part of it. Widows who were well-off often supported ministries and this was the case with Jesus. Luke 8:2-3 says that Mary Magdalene, Joanna, Susanna, and many others provided for Jesus' ministry out of their means.

Although Jesus began his minsitry in Nazareth, he was very quickly rejected. They even tried to kill him for claiming to be the Messiah. So Jesus moved to Capernaum, on the north side of the sea of Galilee, and based his ministry there.

The ruins of Capernaum

As Jesus began his ministry, he gathered a group of followers around him that he took special care to teach and mentor. It was common for gifted religious teachers, such as John the Baptist, to have disciples. Although more people than the disciples eventually traveled with Jesus, only twelve were part of the group we call his disciples.

Nathanael seems to be one of the Twelve but is not mentioned in any of the lists. However, Bartholomew may not be a name so much as a description since "bar means son of and Talmai was a proper name. Nathanael may be the son of Talmai, which would explain his inclusion in the list of the inner circle of Jesus.

The earthly ministry of Jesus was primarily to the Jews. It is only in the context of the Jewish scriptures that we can properly understand who Jesus was, what he taught, and why he had to do what he did. No other culture or religion gives us the proper understanding of Jesus. Even so, Jesus was still rejected by many people who understood what he was saying. But although Jesus can only be understood in a Jewish context, his work and message is for people of all races and all nationalities.

THEOLOGICAL IMPORTANCE

Jesus' ministry spoke to rich and poor, powerful and exploited, men and women, adults and children, Jew and Gentile. He taught about morality, righteousness, justice, and theology. And he taught using sermons, parables, relationships, healings, and miracles. But no matter the setting, audience, or method, Jesus' main message was always his identity. His authority was based on who he was - his identity as the Son of God.

Teachings

Authority

What made Jesus' teachings so startling and controversial is that the way he taught always said something important about himself. The main thing he wanted people to know was who he was, his identity. Jewish religious teachers of the time relied on the authority of the scriptures and tradition. Although Jesus did not deny the Scriptures and followed tradition when it didn't contradict Scripture, he spoke on his own authority and presented his interpretation as authoritative.

By doing this, Jesus was not only teaching that he was the promised Messiah, but that he was God incarnate. Sometimes this is a subtle part of his teaching and sometimes it is very clear, but it is always a part of everything he taught.

Jesus taught in many ways, but how he taught was always tailored to his audience whether it was one person, or a large crowd, or just his disciples. One of the ways Jesus often taught was by telling short stories called parables. These stories used situations and things that were familiar to the mostly poor and rural people that he spoke to—working in the fields, debtors, sheep and goats, lost money, discovered treasure, weddings, and other things from their experience. But the stories always contained a deeper truth about god's kingdom, and the truth was made easier to understand and remember because of the story.

Although Jesus was a great moral teacher, this was not the focus of his ministry. Whether Jesus was teaching about morality or his identity or explaining the Scriptures, the main subject of his teaching was the Kingdom of God. It is this kingdom that the world was created for, and why he came to redeem it. It is this kingdom that he will rule, which is what makes his identity as ruler important. And it is this kingdom that is now being established through his followers.

Content

Methods

Mount of Beatitudes

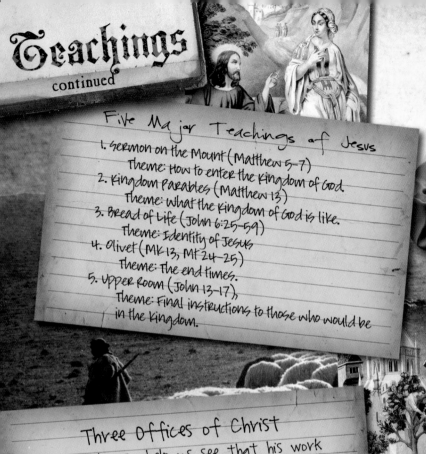

Five Major Teachings of Jesus

1. Sermon on the Mount (Matthew 5-7)
   Theme: How to enter the kingdom of God.
2. Kingdom Parables (Matthew 13)
   Theme: What the kingdom of God is like.
3. Bread of Life (John 6:25-59)
   Theme: Identity of Jesus
4. Olivet (Mk 13, Mt 24-25)
   Theme: The end times.
5. Upper Room (John 13-17),
   Theme: Final instructions to those who would be
   in the kingdom.

Three Offices of Christ

Jesus' teachings help us see that his work
fulfills three offices in the Old Testament
—prophet, priest, and king. He is a prophet
because he brings God's word. He is a priest
because he makes atonement for his people and
intercedes for them on their behalf. And he
is the king whose kingdom is being established
and who will rule forever.

WAYS JESUS REFERRED TO HIMSELF

son of Man
son of God
the door
"I AM"
bread of life
light of the world
the gate

the good shepherd
the resurrection and
the life
the way the truth and
the life
the vine

Jesus spoke of himself in many different ways when he taught. Each way makes an important point about how his identity was the key to understanding his message. No matter how or what he taught he was always teaching about himself. And who he claimed to be in his teachings was what gave him the authority to teach and why we should follow his teachings.

THEOLOGICAL IMPORTANCE

Jesus' teachings are absolutely essential since to be a Christian is to be a follower of Christ, and what is followed are his teachings. But these teachings are not simply things to agree with, or a list of things to do or not do. They are much more. Because of who Jesus is, we should follow his teachings about how we should live. Jesus uses our obedience to establish his kingdom.

Divinity

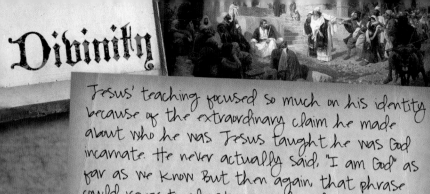

Jesus' teaching focused so much on his identity because of the extraordinary claim he made about who he was Jesus taught he was God incarnate. He never actually said, "I am God" as far as we know But then again, that phrase could refer to almost any god, and is therefore almost meaningless Jesus claimed to be a very specific God. And to make sure he was not misunderstood, he revealed himself to a very specific culture in a very specific way The Jews of Jesus' day did not misunderstand Jesus' claims In fact they understood him perfectly The problem was that many of them didn't believe the claims—that he was the God of Abraham Moses, Isaac, Jacob, and David; the God that had revealed himself through the prophets of the Old Testament.

Another way Jesus claimed to be God was by using names for himself that belong to God or equate him with God. The best example of this is when Jesus refered to himself as "I am," God's personal name for himself. He uses this phrase eight times in John's gospel. One of those times he said, "Before Abraham was, I am" (John 8:58), at which point his audience tried to stone him for blasphemy.

One way Jesus claimed to be God was by doing things that only God is allowed to do and has the power to do. A good example of this is when he told someone that their sins were forgiven. Only God has the power to forgive sins. By saying this, Jesus was claiming to be God. And we know this is how his audience understood him because of how upset they got when they heard him say this.

Several times they picked up stones to kill him since that was the penalty for blasphemy. And when they reacted violently Jesus never tried to tell them that wasn't what he meant.

And Jesus accepted worship, which is also something that only belongs to God. Again, when he was offered worship he accepted it and didn't try to correct a misunderstanding.

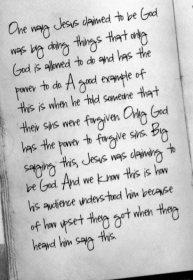

Jesus was not born just as a man who later became God. Nor is Jesus a God who only seemed to be a man. He is not a demi-god, in between man and God. And Jesus is not a mixture of part God and part man. He is also not a human body with a divine spirit. Jesus has a dual nature. He is fully God and fully man at all times. Even now Jesus has a body, though it is different than ours is now because he has been resurrected and has a glorified body. This does not mean that Jesus is not omnipotent, omniscient, omnipresent or all the other things that we know God is. But those things are true only for His divine nature, not his human one. In His divine nature Jesus has always existed. At the incarnation Jesus took on his human nature without change to his divine nature.

The divinity of Jesus is important because it enables him to do for us what we could never do for ourselves. The requirement of God's law is that it be peferctly obeyed, something we can't do because of our fallen nature. And because our sins deserve God's eternal wrath, it takes a person with infinite grace to be able to pay the debt that we owe by taking the punishment we deserve on himself.

Jesus gave Peter, James, and John a glimpse of his divine nature during an event called the Transfiguration. Jesus took these disciples to the top of a mountain where he revealed himself as he will appear in all his glory. It was a picture of how we will see him in the coming kingdom. And just as at Jesus' baptism, God declared, "This is my Son, I take delight in him. Listen to him."

Background: The Mount of Transfiguration

Healings

Jesus healed people of all kinds of illnesses and physical problems. And the more he healed the more his fame spread. People travelled from all over the region to be healed or to ask him to heal someone for them. But often Jesus would ask the person he healed not to tell anyone about him. He knew that people would come to him for the wrong reasons and was trying to make sure they focused on what was important. He wanted them to seek him for who he was—his identity, not what he could do for them.

One reason Jesus healed people was just that they were in need and he had the power to do something about it. And by healing people it showed the kind of person Jesus was. It revealed his character as good, compassionate, and servant-hearted.

Another reason Jesus healed people was to give them a reason to believe things he taught about who he was. For example, when he claimed to forgive the sins of the paralytic lowered through the roof, Jesus was claiming to be God. But his audience did not believe him, especially because anyone can say those words. So to prove he had the power to forgive sin (and was therefore God) he healed the paralytic by telling him to get up and walk. The healing gave people a reason to believe he was telling the truth about whatever he said about himself.

A third reason Jesus healed people was to demonstrate his Lordship over the earth that he will restore and rule over for eternity. His work not only brings redemption for those who believe in him but will undo the curse God placed on creation at the Fall. By healing people Jesus is undoing the curse in a small way that gives us a glimpse of what his completed work will look like and of the kind of power he has over all creation. And this is yet another way in which he is revealing his identity.

Traditional site of the Tomb of Lazarus.

Tyre, where a deaf and mute man was healed in Mark 7:32.

Capernaum, where Jesus healed Peter's mother-in-law.

Background: Pool of Siloam

Pool of Siloam, where Jesus healed a man blind from birth in John 9.

Pool of Bethesda where a bedridden man was healed in John 5:1-18.

Gadarenes, where the demoniac was healed Mt. 8:28-34 & Lk. 8:26-

Cana, where a nobleman's son was healed (Jhn 4:46-54).

THEOLOGICAL IMPORTANCE

Jesus' radical teachings about himself would have sounded like outlandish lies or the talk of a madman if he hadn't given reasons to believe his claims. His miraculous healings are one way he showed he is who he said he is.

Miracles

Jesus also did miracles that weren't healings. But although he did miracles in many different ways and situations, the meaning of them is still the same as his healings: they did some kind of good for people, they pointed to his identity and proved his authority, and they gave a glimpse of his ability to reverse the curse of the Fall when he finally rules his kingdom after he comes again. His miracles were never done without purpose or just to show off his power. These extraordinary events were only used to get people's attention so that they would hear and believe his extraordinary message.

Some miracles show Jesus ruling over nature such as when he walked on water, calmed a storm, fed 5,000, or turned water into wine. By showing his power over the physical world, Jesus was showing us his power over death since the same world he was showing power over is the same world over which death currently reigns. Miracles are a way of Jesus showing that by conquering the world He also conquers death.

Some miracles Jesus did can be described as miracles of timing. An example would be in Luke 5:11 when he tells his disciples to throw their nets in the water after they'd just spent the night catching nothing. When they did, they caught so many fish they needed help to keep the boat from sinking under the weight. Nature did not behave any differently than normal. This kind of miracle shows that Jesus (in his divine nature) has the power to know the appointed times of events.

THEOLOGICAL IMPORTANCE

When God chose to speak through a prophet he gave them a sign, a miracle that they would do to prove they truly were a prophet. Anyone who claimed to be a prophet but did not show a sign was not only rejected but put to death. Jesus' miracles prove he is who he said he is.

Miracles
continued

A miracle is when God acts in an unusual way to reveal himself. A miracle is different from providence, which is how God normally works in the universe. God upholds the entire universe and nothing happens in it that is beyond his control. To do this, he either acts directly or he uses something else through which to do his work. For example, gravity would be something God creates to do his work of keeping order in the physical universe. The laws of nature describe the regularity of the universe, and the regularity of the universe is due to God's providence. But this regularity is what lets us recognize when something unusual happens in it, and that is what a miracle is.

Miracles are not a violation of the laws of nature, nor do they deny science. Science describes the normal workings of the world and makes predictions about how it will work in the future because of the regularity of the universe. But when scientists make these predictions they don't consider what happens if a person enters into the equation by making a choice. For example, the law of gravity tells us an apple will fall from the tree towards the ground. But it cannot tell us if someone will reach out and catch it.

So when God chooses to reveal himself in a miraculous way, it is not something that science can be the judge of since it is happening outside of what science investigates. To say that there is no scientific proof for a miracle doesn't mean the miracle didn't happen because miracles are not the kinds of things that can be measured by science.

Some philosophers have said that an intelligent person should not believe in miracles because our experience says that most people don't claim to have seen a miracle. Also, if miracles do exist then they are so rare and unlikely that the best thing to do is reject any miracle claim. The problem is that just because something has never happened to you and is rare does not mean it is logical to deny it happened. Think about George Washington, for example. He died long before any of us were born, so he is not part of our experience. And in the entire course of history, he lived only once. Does that really mean we should deny George Washington ever existed? Of course not! The argument against miracles fails, for exactly the same reasons.

Cana, where Jesus turned water to wine.

Enemies

It can be hard to think of Jesus as having enemies. And yet there were many people who opposed him, some of them violently. His teaching about himself is what led his enemies to want to kill him. By understanding why the enemies of Jesus were threatened by him we can learn more about Jesus himself.

The House of Caiaphas, the High Priest

The Sadducees were the religious leaders in Jerusalem and controlled the Jewish court called the Sanhedrin. They thought scripture only contained the five books of Moses, and they did not believe in the resurrection of the dead at the final judgment. They were most interested in political power and used their religious positions to attain it. They felt very threatened by Jesus and were the ones who began the plot to have him arrested and killed.

The Pharisees were the religious leaders in the synagogues, which were places that congregations outside of Jerusalem met for teaching. Their scripture contained the same books as in our Old Testament. They were so focused on earning righteousness on their own that they invented all sorts of laws and traditions that they thought helped them keep God's law better. Jesus rejected their man-made traditions and their attempts to justify themselves. In the eyes of the Pharisees, Jesus broke the law of Moses and was a blasphemer. And his opposition was a threat to their position as religious leaders. However, some Pharisees became followers of Jesus.

Ruins of a synagogue in Capernaum

The Fortress of Antonia, part of the Roman headquarters in Jerusalem.

The Romans were mainly interested in keeping the peace in the region. They didn't care about a religious disagreement between Jesus and the Jewish leaders, so the governor of Judea, Pontius Pilate, didn't want to get involved. But when the Jewish leaders told Pilate that Jesus claimed to be a king and was therefore a threat to the emperor, Pilate had to act. At first he found Jesus not guilty and tried to let him go, but the Jews insisted Jesus be crucified. And when the Jews hinted that Caesar would be told that Pilate let someone claiming to be king go, Pilate was forced to give the order for Jesus to be executed. So three groups who were normally enemies of each other found a reason to join together and stand against Jesus.

Jesus' most powerful enemy was Satan. It was Satan's influence that led to the Fall of Adam and Eve and the curse that resulted. And it is in Genesis 3:15 that we get our first glimpse of the Gospel since Jesus is the seed who has come to crush the serpent's head. Satan tempted Jesus to skip all of the trials and suffering of this life and become king if Jesus would just worship him. Satan knew that Jesus' victory on the cross would mean the beginning of the reversal of the curse and the end of Satan's reign. He knew that Jesus' death and resurrection would mean he would be defeated and that at the final judgment he would receive God's full wrath in a place where he could never again influence the world.

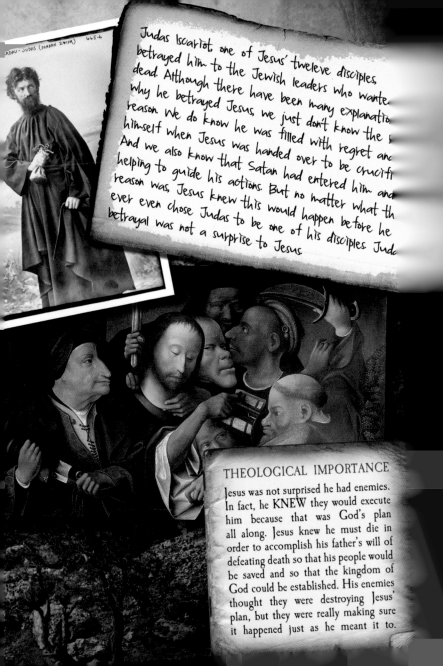

Judas Iscariot, one of Jesus' tweleve disciples, betrayed him to the Jewish leaders who wante_ dead. Although there have been many explanatio_ why he betrayed Jesus, we just don't know the _ reason. We do know he was filled with regret an_ himself when Jesus was handed over to be crucifi_ And we also know that Satan had entered him an_ helping to guide his actions. But no matter what th_ reason was, Jesus knew this would happen before he _ ever even chose Judas to be one of his disciples. Jud_ betrayal was not a surprise to Jesus.

THEOLOGICAL IMPORTANCE

Jesus was not surprised he had enemies. In fact, he KNEW they would execute him because that was God's plan all along. Jesus knew he must die in order to accomplish his father's will of defeating death so that his people would be saved and so that the kingdom of God could be established. His enemies thought they were destroying Jesus' plan, but they were really making sure it happened just as he meant it to.

Triumphal Entry

The way Jesus chose to enter Jerusalem when he knew that he would be killed is extremely important. Although he travelled on foot most of the way there, he stopped not far from Jerusalem and sent for a donkey that he could ride the rest of the way. He did this to fulfil the prophecy of Zechariah 9:9 which says the Messiah will come humbly riding into Jerusalem on a donkey. The people who saw him understood that Jesus was claiming to be the long-awaiting Messiah, so they lined the road with their cloaks or palm branches. As he passed by, the crowd cried out "Hosanna!" which means "The Lord saves!" His arrival also completed the 69th week, the time foretold in Daniel 9 for the arrival of the Messiah. When Jesus proclaimed his identity as Messiah at the Triumphal Entry, he was officially presenting himself before the Jewish rulers for the last time.

The Golden Gate, where Jesus enter Jerusalem at his Triumphal Entry.

The road Jesus may have travelled on his way to the Golden Gate.

THEOLOGICAL IMPORTANCE

When Jesus entered Jerusalem he wasn't simply arriving in town. The way in which he entered was a statement that he was presenting himself to Israel as the long-awaited Messiah. At the Last Supper Jesus instituted the signs of the New Covenant and prepared the Twelve for what to do after he was gone. Jesus' betrayal fulfilled prophecy that identified him as the Messiah. And his trials were the formal rejection of the Messiah by the Jewish leaders.

Background: Gethsemane

Last Supper

A medieval building built on the traditional site of the Upper Room

The Last Supper was the celebration of the third and final Passover of Jesus' ministry. Jesus arranged to have a guest room prepared by having Peter and John enter Jerusalem and follow the man they saw carrying water (an unusual thing for a man to do at that time) to his house. By giving such strange instructions to only two of the disciples, Jesus kept Judas from knowing where they would be that night. During the Passover feast, Jesus revealed that he would be betrayed. After encouraging Judas to leave, Jesus gave one of his major teachings and talked about the new responsibilities believers would have when he returned to the Father. He also instituted the sacrament of the Lord's Supper, a picture of the Gospel believers were to use to remember Christ's work and identity. Jesus also knew that as he spoke Judas was reporting his whereabouts to the Jewish leaders. But before they could return and arrest him at the supper, Jesus and his disciples left for the Garden of Gethsemane. Jesus was in complete control of the events and timing of his arrest, trial, and execution. Judas probably returned to an empty room and then guessed Jesus was headed for the Mount of Olives for the night like he usually did. This gave Jesus more time with his disciples and time in prayer to prepare himself for the difficult final hours that lay ahead of him.

...anal

The Garden of Gethsemane where Jesus was arrested.

...upper, Jesus spent time in prayer in the ...mane. Although Jesus knew his mission ...ie a sacrificial death on the cross, ... a way to accomplish the same goal ...he cross. It wasn't only the physical ...wanted to avoid, he mainly wanted to ... from the Father that must take ... punishment for our sin. But what ...was to do his Father's will, so he ...death.

Traditional spot of the Betrayal.

411 Spot of the Betrayal. Bruthen gelten. Kocher des Apôtres.

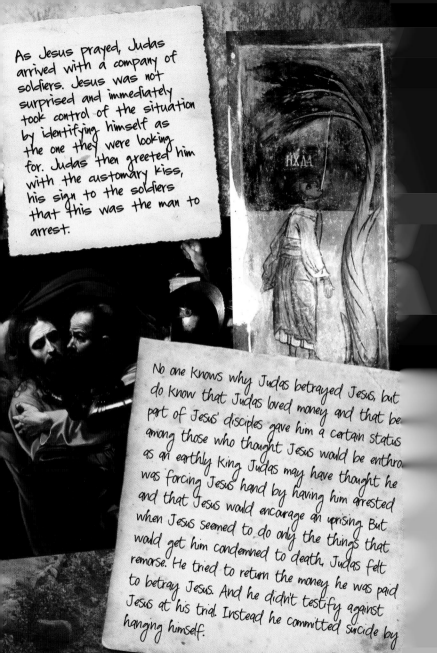

As Jesus prayed, Judas arrived with a company of soldiers. Jesus was not surprised and immediately took control of the situation by identifying himself as the one they were looking for. Judas then greeted him with the customary kiss, his sign to the soldiers that this was the man to arrest.

ΗΧΑΑ

No one knows why Judas betrayed Jesus, but do know that Judas loved money and that be part of Jesus' disciples gave him a certain status among those who thought Jesus would be enthro as an earthly King. Judas may have thought he was forcing Jesus' hand by having him arrested and that Jesus would encourage an uprising. But when Jesus seemed to do only the things that would get him condemned to death, Judas felt remorse. He tried to return the money he was paid to betray Jesus. And he didn't testify against Jesus at his trial. Instead he committed suicide by hanging himself.

Trials

After his arrest, Jesus was tried six times over the next few hours. The first three trials were religious, and the second three were civil trials. The first trial was a hearing before Annas, a former high priest who still held enormous power and was the father-in-law of the current high priest, Caiaphas. They may have broght Jesus to Annas to make sure they should go ahead with the plan to find a way to kill Jesus. Annas felt insulted by Jesus' answers and sent him on to Caiaphas and the Sanhedrin.

The Sanhedrin was the group of religious leaders who governed the Jews in religious matters. Although there were both Sadduccees and Pharisees, the Sadduccees usually had more power. When Jesus was brought before the Sanhedrin it was around 2 or 3 in the morning and only some of the Sanhedrin were there. The trial was disorganized because they were scrambling for witnesses to testify against Jesus. They probably thought Judas would provide evidence but his remorse led him to back out of the whole process. Finally Jesus was asked directly whether or not he was the Son of God. Jesus not only said he was, but he then quoted Daniel 7:13 as referring to himself—a messianic verse. Caiaphas tore his robes in response to this apparent blashpemy and a death sentence was given shortly after that.

Just after dawn, the full Sanhedrin met. They brought Jesus forward and confirmed the death sentence. But under Roman rule they couldn't carry out the sentence, so they sent Jesus to the Roman governor Pontius' Pilate.

Jesus' fourth trial was before Pontius Pilate. Although the Sanhedrin wanted Jesus put to death for blasphemy, they changed the charge before Pilate to sedition. Jesus had claimed to be a king. And because Rome could only have one king, Jesus was to be seen as a threat to the empire. Pilate did not find enough evidence to convict Jesus and was looking for a way out of a potentially messy political situation. When the Jews mentioned Jesus was from Galilee, Pilate took advantage of the situation and sent Jesus to King Herod.

Herod had heard many things about Jesus and was very anxious to meet him. But when Jesus appeared before him, Herod was only interested in seeing Jesus work a miracle for his own entertainment. When Jesus refused, Herod sent him back to Pilate.

At Jesus' sixth trial Pilate realized that the Jews could start a riot if the situation wasn't dealt with quickly. Pilate tried to quiet the crowd by offering to release a prisoner to them. But given the choice between Jesus and Barabbas (a man actually guilty of insurrection) the crowd not only demanded Barabbas be released, but they still wanted Jesus crucified. Wanting to keep the peace, Pilate handed over Jesus to be crucified. But before doing so, he washed his hands as a sign that he considered himself innocent in the death of Jesus.

The Praetorium, where Jesus appeared before Pilate.

Death

The exact date of Jesus' death isn't known with certainty, but there are enough clues to give us two possible days. Herod the Great died in 4 B.C. and Jesus was born within two years of that, making his birth 4–6 B.C. Luke dates the time that John the Baptist began his ministry as the 15th year of Tiberius Caesar. Tiberius began to rule with his father before taking over sole authority at his father's death, so Luke could mean one of two dates. His father Augustus died in A.D. 14.

If A.D. 14 is the date Luke meant, then John began his ministry in AD 28 or 29. If he meant the time Tiberius began to rule with his father then the year would be 26 or 27. This earlier date works a bit better with the other things we know about Jesus' life. Luke says Jesus began his ministry at about 30 years old. That puts Jesus' ministry beginning in A.D. 27. When we add in the three Passovers John said Jesus celebrated during his ministry, we arrive at A.D. 30. as the year of his death.

Jesus was crucified at 9a.m. on the morning of Nisan 15. At 12p.m. the sky turned dark for three hours. Jesus died at 3p.m. If the A.D. 30 date is correct then when we place it on our calendar we can date the crucifixion of Christ as happening on April 7, AD 30.

Interestingly, the two best reckonings of the appearance of the messiah as prophecied by Daniel 9's 70 weeks lead us to April 7, AD 30 or April 3, AD 33.

According to the Gospels, Jesus was crucified on what the Jews called the "Day of Preparation," which meant Friday since they were preparing for the Sabbath. The date of the Passover meal was always the evening of the 14th of Nisan on the Jewish calendar. This fell on a Thursday in A.D. 30 and A.D. 33, which makes them the only two possibilities for the year of Jesus' crucifixion. The A.D. 33 date, however, would either make Jesus' ministry a couple of years longer than we can date using scripture, or he was a little older than we think when he began his ministry.

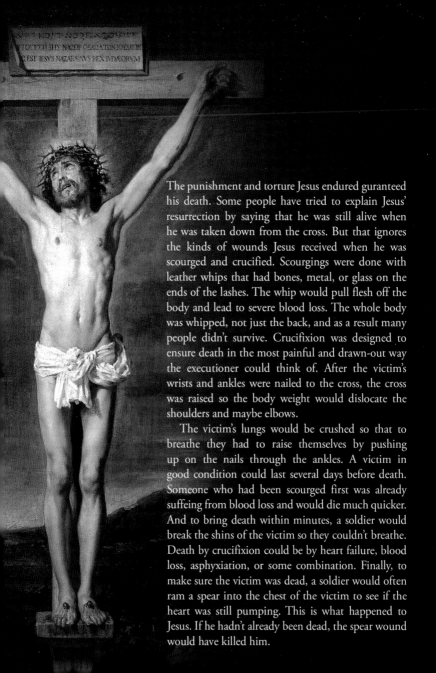

The punishment and torture Jesus endured guranteed his death. Some people have tried to explain Jesus' resurrection by saying that he was still alive when he was taken down from the cross. But that ignores the kinds of wounds Jesus received when he was scourged and crucified. Scourgings were done with leather whips that had bones, metal, or glass on the ends of the lashes. The whip would pull flesh off the body and lead to severe blood loss. The whole body was whipped, not just the back, and as a result many people didn't survive. Crucifixion was designed to ensure death in the most painful and drawn-out way the executioner could think of. After the victim's wrists and ankles were nailed to the cross, the cross was raised so the body weight would dislocate the shoulders and maybe elbows.

The victim's lungs would be crushed so that to breathe they had to raise themselves by pushing up on the nails through the ankles. A victim in good condition could last several days before death. Someone who had been scourged first was already suffeing from blood loss and would die much quicker. And to bring death within minutes, a soldier would break the shins of the victim so they couldn't breathe. Death by crucifixion could be by heart failure, blood loss, asphyxiation, or some combination. Finally, to make sure the victim was dead, a soldier would often ram a spear into the chest of the victim to see if the heart was still pumping. This is what happened to Jesus. If he hadn't already been dead, the spear wound would have killed him.

Burial

Around AD 135, Hadrian put down the second Jewish revolt and tried to erase from the city anything having to do with their history. One of the things he did was to fill in the quarry that held what Christians believed was Jesus' tomb. Hadrian built a temple to Roman gods on top of the quarry. Two hundred years later or so, Constantine's mother, Helena, travelled to Jerusalem and was shown the temple and told its history. Because Christians had lived in the city continuously since the crucifixion, the site was remembered. It turns out that instead of erasing the site as he had intended, Hadrian's actions had marked it. Constantine ordered an excavation and soon the tombs were found. Apparently one of them was distinguished from the others as Jesus' tomb (possibly by graffiti of those who wished to mark the tomb originally) and a church was built around it. Although many additions have been made, and although it has been knocked down, burned, and restored many times, evidence of Constantine's church can still be found as well as the foundation of Hadrian's temple. Most of the original tomb traditionally said to be Jesus' has been destroyed, though the bench and part of one wall are probably original. There is no way to know if the traditional tomb of Jesus really is the tomb he was buried in. But there is good reason to believe that these are the actual burial grounds of Jesus.

Entrance to the Church of the Holy Sepulchre

Joseph of Arimathea, a member of the Sanhedrin who was a follower of Jesus, asked Pilate for Jesus' body. Joseph, with the help of Nicodemus, buried Jesus according to Jewish custom. Mary Magdalene and the other Mary were there as well. The cheif priests were afraid that Jesus' followers would steal his body and claim that he was risen from the dead. So Pilate gave them soldiers to guard the tomb.

THEOLOGICAL IMPORTANCE

Jesus' death on the cross didn't take him by surprise. It wasn't an accident or bad luck. In fact, Jesus not only didn't avoid his death, he orchestrated the timing and circumstances. He knew he was born to die, and he gave his life willingly. Jesus knew that he didn't come to earth to simply be our good example. He knew his purpose was far bigger than that—it was a rescue mission. Because of Adam's sin in the garden of Eden, all people are born with a sinful nature. And because of their sinful natures, all people deserve death. God is holy, righteous, and just, and cannot let sin go unpunished, and the punishment is death. But God is also a loving God and loved the world so much that he gave his one and only son to take on human flesh, live a perfect life, and take the punishment of his people in their place. He died in the place of those who believe in him. When he died, he received the punsihment they justly deserved. And believers in him received the righteousness he earned. Only blood can atone for sin. That's why God established animal sacrifice as part of the worship he required prior to Jesus' death. But the death of the animals sacrificed were only a promise that pointed forward to a time when a sacrifice would be made once and for all. A perfect sacrifice that removed the need for any more blood to be shed. And that sacrifice was Jesus. Those who believe in him are judged by his works of perfect righteousness and our sins have been paid for by the punishment taken on by Jesus, and as a result we are forgiven. Jesus did for us what we could not do for ourselves - he earned God's favor through perfect obedience. Jesus was well aware that without his obedience to undergo this death no one could be saved. All were lost. The cross is God's sending Jesus on a rescue mission to save his people. Salvation is not anything we earn but something Jesus earned for those who would believe in him. And it is a gift freely given to all who ask for it.

Resurrection

After appearing to the women, Jesus appeared to two of his followers on their way to Emmaus. They were confused and saddened at Jesus' death. Jesus hid his identy from them as they travelled together, but spent the time explaining the scriptures and how he fulfilled the promises God had made to his people. When he finally revealed himself, he disappeared.

THEOLOGICAL IMPORTANCE

How do we know that Jesus was telling the truth about who he was and what he came to do? How do we know that his death on the cross paid for the sins of those who believe in him? Why should we believe that his perfect righteousness has been credited to his followers? The answer is because of the Resurrection. Jesus made many predictions about his death - who would betray him, who would condemn him, when, and where it would happen. But most outrageously, he claimed that on the third day after his death he would be raised from the dead. If Jesus was telling the truth about that then we have good reason to believe everything he said.

Background: First century tomb

At dawn on Sunday morning, on the third day after Jesus' death, several of his women followers, including Mary Magdalene, visited the tomb to anoint his body with spices. But they found that the stone sealing the entrance had been rolled away, and Jesus' body was gone. Instead they saw an angel who told them that Jesus had risen just as he said he would. The angel also told them to go tell the disciples. They were terrified by what was happening, but did as the angel said and ran to tell the disciples. Mary Magdalene found Peter and John. They didn't believe her, but they ran to the tomb to investigate what happened. They also found the tomb empty, but they didn't meet the angel. After Peter and John left, Mary remained behind crying at the tomb. As she was mourning, Jesus appeared to her. Then he appeared to the rest of the women, who had found the empty tomb.

The discovery of the empty tomb by women, and that they were the first people to encounter the risen Jesus, is extremely important. In that culture and at that time women were very poorly treated and did not have the same social or legal standing as men. They weren't allowed to testify in a court of law, or if they did then their testimony wasn't taken seriously. This means the central claim of the Christian faith relies on witnesses whose testimony would not be allowed in court. This is an indication that this event really happened. If the story was invented then we'd expect to see the tomb discovered by the MOST reliable witnesses (Peter, James, or John), not the least reliable witnesses.

Resurrection

Jesus appeared to his disciples many times in many different situations for 40 days. He gave them powerful reasons to believe in him and instructions for what to do with that belief as a special group of people trained for the special purpose of spreading the Good News about himself. Although his body was physical, it was now glorified. It couldn't die again, couldn't get sick or suffer harm, and it would never be hungry. This is the kind of body his followers will be resurrected to when Jesus comes again as he promised. His glorified body is not only our proof of his payment for our sins, but shows how Jesus' death and resurrection reverses the curse put on the world as a result of Adam's sin.

The disciples were so convinced they had encountered the risen Jesus that they radically changed their lives as a result. They split up and travelled as far as Britain, Ethiopia, and possibly India in order to spread the gospel of Jesus Christ. They gave up the comforts of home and whatever security they had in order to proclaim the truth they had been entrusted with. In return they were persecuted, beaten, jailed, and with one exception (John) brutally martyred for teaching Jesus was the one true God. They didn't act like conspirators who had invented the story. And although they had plenty of opportunity to admit to making up the story as they were tortured and killed, not one of them confessed to doing so. In other words, they acted like people telling the truth.

Background: First century tomb

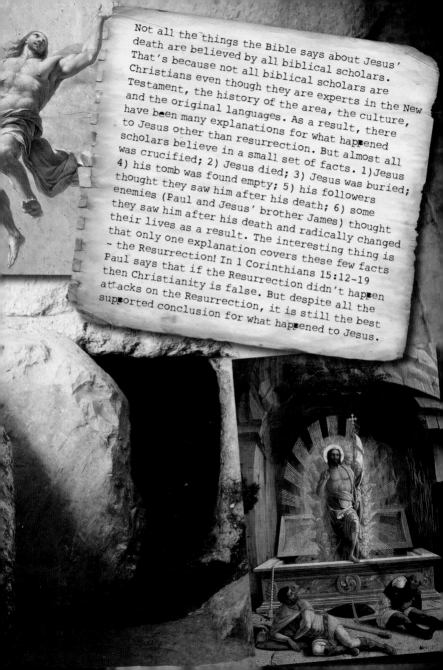

Not all the things the Bible says about Jesus' death are believed by all biblical scholars. That's because not all biblical scholars are Christians even though they are experts in the New Testament, the history of the area, the culture, and the original languages. As a result, there have been many explanations for what happened to Jesus other than resurrection. But almost all scholars believe in a small set of facts. 1)Jesus was crucified; 2) Jesus died; 3) Jesus was buried; 4) his tomb was found empty; 5) his followers thought they saw him after his death; 6) some enemies (Paul and Jesus' brother James) thought they saw him after his death and radically changed their lives as a result. The interesting thing is that only one explanation covers these few facts – the Resurrection! In 1 Corinthians 15:12-19 Paul says that if the Resurrection didn't happen then Christianity is false. But despite all the attacks on the Resurrection, it is still the best supported conclusion for what happened to Jesus.

Ascension

The Ascension of Jesus into Heaven is sometimes overlooked as a footnote to his resurrection. But it's a very significant event in Jesus' ministry. After appearing to his followers for 40 days, Jesus took his disciples to the Mount of Olives. He gave them some final instructions, and then he ascended into the sky before being hidden by the clouds. When Jesus ascended he finally received the glory and honor that was his. It had been his before his incarnation, but he set it aside when he became a man. He never stopped being fully God during his time on earth, but he did set aside the glory and honor due him. The Ascension shows him for the first time receiving this glory and honor as someone who was fully God and fully man. When he returns he will come as he left — in the clouds. The only difference is that at that time everyone will see him in his exalted state as he wields his power in judgment, and as he consumates his reign over the Kingdom of God once and for all

Traditional spot of the ascension.

Once in heaven, Jesus sat down at the right hand of the Father. This is important because it means Jesus' work of redemption was completed. It is not incomplete, insufficient, or ongoing in any way. His work is finished, and that means the salvation of those who believe in him is secured. Their salvation cannot be undone and it is not in question. Jesus' ascension gives us assurance of our pardon for our sins and assurance of our salvation. Because of his ascension, the Holy Spirit can now do his work of testifying to the finished work of Jesus Christ.

The Ascension also reminds us that Jesus has a human body that is in a specific place even now. In his divine nature, Jesus has no location since he is omnipresent. But in his human nature he can be in only one place at a time. The Ascension of his physical body gives us a glimpse of what it will be like when we (his believers) are resurrected and dwell in his presence. It's not just a good story—it's a promised reality for those who trust in him.

THEOLOGICAL IMPORTANCE

When Jesus ascended into Heaven he was seen clearly as fully God and fully man because he received the glory and honor that is reserved for God alone. It was his final teaching that he is the Messiah, the one and only mediator between God and man. There is no other way to God than through faith in Jesus Christ.

Background: Jerusalem from the Mount of Olives

In Mark 8:29 Jesus asks his disciples, "Who do you say I am?" But this question wasn't just for his disciples. It is for us as well. And how we answer this question has eternal consequences. Was Jesus simply our good example? Was Jesus nothing more than a great moral teacher? Was Jesus the greatest con-man who ever lived? Was he a misunderstood rabbi who became a victim when things got out of control? Was he an insane man whose delusions were taken seriously by some people? Or was he who he said he was—God incarnate who came to die for the sins of those who would believe in him? Who do YOU say he is?

"I am the way, the truth, and the life. No one comes to the Father except through Me."
John 14:6

IMAGES

Intro
iStockphoto: vintage label.

Annunciation
CC-by-SA Unported 3.0: Caesar by Marsyas;
Paintings (L-R): Fra Angelico, Don Lorenzo
Monaco;

Birth
Dreamstime: calendar page; Library of Congress:
map; Painting: Dürer.

Baptism
Paintings (L-R): Dürer, Millais, Hunt.

Temptations
Paintings: Meister des Hitda, Nelkenmeister,
Iwanow, Flandes, Kramskoi, Thoma.

Ministry
Library of Congress: map; iStockphoto: scroll;
Public Domain: 12 apostles - photo: Ib Rasmussen;
Painting: Fra Angelico

Teachings
Paintings (L-R): Rembrandt, Kirchebner, Tissot;
Public Domain: photo of painting of Jesus with
the Children by Andreas Praefcke; CC-by-SA 3.0
Unported: Statue of jesus - Photo by: Raymac;
Library of Congtress: book covers.

Divinity
iStockphoto: rocks; Paintings and Engraving
(L-R): Rode, Semiradsky, Meister des
Universitäts-Altars; CC-by-SA 3.0 Unported:
Jesus icon photo: Rh-67, Trinity illustration
photo: Przykuta.

Healings
Paintings (L-R): Veronese, Hitda, El Greco;

Miracles
Dreamstime: loaves and fish; Paintings (L-R):
Aivazovsky, Rembrandt, Raphael, Veronese.

Enemies
Paintings: Crivelli, Bosch, Munkácsy,
Mantegna; CC-bySA 3.0-Unported: Lucifer
photo: Luc Viatour.

Triumphal Entry / Betrayal / Trials
Paintings (L-R): Poussin, Ge; CC-by-SA
3.0-Unported: Caiaphas - photo: Joseolgon.

Death / Burial
Paintings: Peterzano, Velázquez.

Resurrection
Paintings (L-R); Fra Angelico, Führich,
Mantegna, Rembrandt; CC-by-SA 3.0-Unported:
icon of resurrection - photo: Schiwago.

Ascension
Paintings: Cosimo, Obrazopisov; CC-by-SA
2.0: icon photo by ACOR Cannes; CC-by-SA
3.0-Unported: sculture of Christ.

Credits / divider
Photo of tomb: Public Domain
Painting: Caravaggio

All vintage photos and uncredited art is in
the public domain.

All paper scraps and photo borders from
iStockphoto, Dreamstime, SXC, or the Library
of Congress.

BIBLIOGRAPHY

Carson, D.A., Douglas J. Moo, Leon
Morris, *An Introduction to the New
Testament* (Grand Rapids: Zondervan,
1992).

Grudem, Wayne, *Systematic Theology*
(Grand Rapids: Zondervan, 1994).

Howard, Jeremy Royal, *Holman
QuickSource Guide to Understanding
Jesus* (Nashville: B&H, 2009).

Thomas, Robert L., Stanley N.
Gundry, *A Harmony of the Gospels* (San
Francisco: HarperSanFrancisco, 1978,
1991).

THANKS

Jeremy Howard, Jeff Godby, David Owen
Filson, Zan Tyler, Davis Carman,
Jules, Mia.

In this passage, Paul says that if there is a better explanation for what happened to Jesus three days after his death and burial then Christians have wasted their time and their lives. Paul believed so strongly in the evidence for the historical, bodily resurrection of Jesus that he actually points out the place where enemies and skeptics should attack Christianity if they are trying to defeat it. But is the historical, bodily resurrection of Jesus really the best way to understand the evidence?

Now if Christ is proclaimed as raised from the dead, how can some of you say, "There is no resurrection of the dead"? But if there is no resurrection of the dead, then Christ has not been raised; and if Christ has not been raised, then our proclamation is without foundation, and so is your faith. In addition, we are found to be false witnesses about God, because we have testified about God that He raised up Christ—whom He did not raise up if in fact the dead are not raised. For if the dead are not raised, Christ has not been raised. And if Christ has not been raised, your faith is worthless; you are still in your sins. Therefore, those who have fallen asleep in Christ have also perished. If we have put our hope in Christ for this life only, we should be pitied more than anyone.

1 Corinthians 15:12-19

Predictions by Jesus about his Death

The historical, bodily resurrection of Jesus is extremely important because it proves he can be trusted. During his life on Earth, Jesus said many things that were difficult to believe or prove. Some of these claims were about himself—who he was and what his authority was. Jesus taught that he was God. And not just any god, but the one, true God who had revealed himself through Abraham, Moses, David and other prophets. In fact, the reason Jesus was executed was for teaching that he was God. But how do we know if Jesus was telling the truth about himself? Jesus knew our problem and gave us a solution. He made predictive prophecies about who would put him to death, how they would treat him, how they would get to him, when they would do it, where he would die, and—most astonishingly—that he would be raised from the dead on the third day. If there is evidednce that he was in fact resurrected on the third day then we have good reason to believe that Jesus was telling us the truth about everything else he said. The resurrection is how we know Jesus can be trusted.

suffer at the hands of the elders, chief priests, and scribes, be killed, and be raised on the third day

From then on Jesus began to point out to His disciples that He must go to Jerusalem and suffer many things from the elders, chief priests, and scribes, be killed and be raised on the third day. **Matthew 16:21**

Then He began to teach them that the Son of Man must suffer many things and be rejected by the elders, the chief priests, and the scribes, be killed, and rise after three days. **Mark 8:31**

For He was teaching His disciples and telling them, "The Son of Man is being betrayed into the hands of men. They will kill Him, and after He is killed, He will rise three days later." **Mark 9:31**

"Listen! We are going up to Jerusalem. The Son of Man will be handed over to the chief priests and the scribes, and they will condemn Him to death. Then they will hand Him over to the Gentiles, and they will mock Him, spit on Him, flog Him, and kill Him, and He will rise after three days." **Mark 10:33-34**

"But after I have been resurrected, I will go ahead of you to Galilee." **Mark 14:28**

Then He took the Twelve aside and told them, "Listen! We are going up to Jerusalem. Everything that is written through the prophets about the Son of Man will be accomplished. For He will be handed over to the Gentiles, and He will be mocked, insulted, spit on; and after they flog Him, they will kill Him, and He will rise on the third day."

LUKE 18:31-33

Predictions continued

While they were eating, He said, "I assure you: One of you will betray Me."

Matthew 26:21

While they were reclining and eating, Jesus said, "I assure you: One of you will betray Me—one who is eating with Me!"

Mark 14:18

"But look, the hand of the one betraying Me is at the table with Me!"

Luke 22:21

"But the Scripture must be fulfilled: The one who eats My bread has raised his heel against Me. I am telling you now before it happens, so that when it does happen you will believe that I am He."...When Jesus had said this, He was troubled in His spirit and testified, "I assure you: One of you will betray Me!"

John 13:18b-19, 21

Betrayal

TIME OF DEATH

Jesus replied to them, "The hour has come for the Son of Man to be glorified."

John 12:23

THE MINIMAL FACTS

Although Jesus gave us prophecies to help us understand him correctly, not all scholars of the New Testament agree on how the events and claims of Jesus' life and death should be interpreted. Not only that, but not all scholars agree on what the historical facts about Jesus are and where they come from. This is because there are many kinds of beliefs that scholars have; some are atheists, some believe a non-Christian religion, some are liberal Christians, and some believe historic, orthodox Christianity.

However, when they write about Jesus' resurrection, there are a few facts (called the minimal facts) that almost all New Testament scholars agree on. These facts are found in more than one writing, were believed by enemies of Christianity, come from an eyewitness report, come from a time soon after Jesus' death, and/or could be embarassing for Christianity. What is interesting about this is that only the biblical account of the resurrection makes sense of these few facts. No other explanation covers them all. The next few pages show the six minimal facts. Then we'll see how different explanations of what happened to Jesus after his death each fail to account for these facts. All except the historical, bodily resurrection.

Crucified
and Died

THE FACTS

Jesus was crucified.

Jesus died on the cross.

Roman Nail
from the
1st century
that might
be like the
ones used in
crucifixion.

CRUCIFIXION

Nails in wrists hold body upright and cause extreme pain. Hands are probably partially parylized from nerve damage.

- Nail(s) through feet or ankle(s) holds weight and gives victim something to push on.

- Shoulders and elbows may dislocate from weight of body, making arms almost useless.

- Victim's weight forces victim to inhale and makes exhalation very difficult.

- Victim must relieve weight in order to exhale by pushing up on nail(s) in ankle(s) and pulling down on nails in wrists.

- Wounds on back scrape against the post with every breath and therefore remain open.

Death occurs as a result of many things, such as shock from blood loss, asphyxiation, congestive heart failure, and dehydration. If the victim was in good condition he could live for several days on the cross. Others died in hours. If Roman soldiers wanted someone to die quickly they would break the shins of the victim so they could no longer push up to exhale. Once the legs were broken, death would come within minutes.

Even though the Romans crucified thousands of people, there is almost no archaeological evidence of it. That's because many victims were left on the cross to rot as a kind of gruesome warning. Victims taken down from the cross were buried in a common grave.

There is only one historical account of someone surviving crucifixion but that victim was taken down to be rescued and had his wounds treated. Two others taken down at the same time still died from their wounds. Roman soldiers carrying out the executions made sure everyone who was supposed to die actually did die.

Although it was unusual, in some cases the bodies were given back to a family or friend so a proper burial could be given. In the late 1960's the skeleton of a crucifixion victim who was buried properly was found in Jerusalem. One of the ankles still had a nail running through it and the wrists show signs of being worn down by hanging from a nail.

Crucified Continued and Died

Before being crucified, Jesus was scourged with a whip called a flagrum. Flagrums had several chords with metal balls on the end and often had shards of bone, metal, or rocks in them as well. Scourging was designed to pull flesh off the victim. Some victims did not survive.

To make sure Jesus was dead, a soldier pierced Jesus through the side and into the heart. If Jesus had not already died, he would have died from the spear wound.

The Man in the Shroud of Turin

The Shroud of Turin is a long piece of linen kept in a church in Turin, Italy, that many people believe is the cloth Jesus was wrapped in when he was buried. In addition to blood stains, there is a very faint image on the cloth of a man. But this image can't be seen well unless a photo is taken and reversed. The negative image reveals that the man has the same wounds that Jesus would have had after being scourged, crucified, and speared in the side.

Some tests on the shroud have dated it to the Middle Ages, which would mean it's a fake. But other tests and additional information found on the shroud indicate the shroud is much older. In the end, we don't know if this is Jesus' burial cloth or not. What we do know is that the man in the shroud suffered in the same way as Jesus.

the Empty Tomb

Only a very few of the most liberal scholars do not believe Jesus was buried. They believe he was either left on the cross to rot or thrown into a shallow, unmarked grave.

THE FACTS

Jesus was buried in a tomb. Three days after Jesus was buried his tomb was found empty. The body was gone.

A first century tomb in Israel similar to the one Jesus was buried in. Inside there may be one or several places to lay a body.

Traditional site of Jesus' tomb as it appears today.

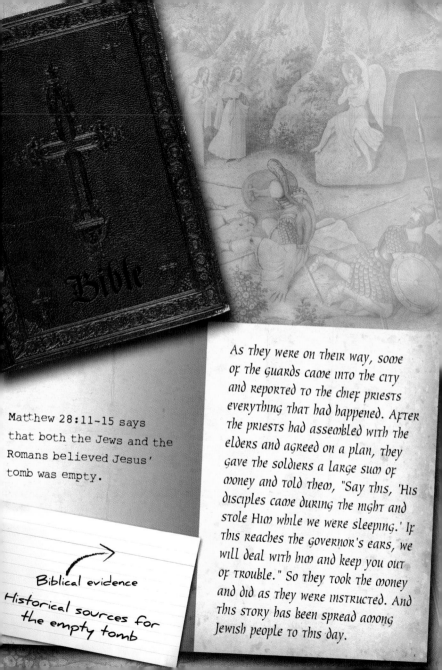

Matthew 28:11-15 says that both the Jews and the Romans believed Jesus' tomb was empty.

Biblical evidence
Historical sources for the empty tomb

As they were on their way, some of the guards came into the city and reported to the chief priests everything that had happened. After the priests had assembled with the elders and agreed on a plan, they gave the soldiers a large sum of money and told them, "Say this, 'His disciples came during the night and stole Him while we were sleeping.' If this reaches the governor's ears, we will deal with him and keep you out of trouble." So they took the money and did as they were instructed. And this story has been spread among Jewish people to this day.

the Empty Tomb

Continued

Justin Martyr

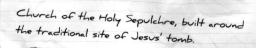

Church of the Holy Sepulchre, built around the traditional site of Jesus' tomb.

Church Father Justin Martyr wrote a book around AD 150 called *Dialogue with Trypho*. In chapter 108 he reports that the Jews taught Jesus' body was stolen, which means they believed his tomb was empty.

"(The Jews) have sent chosen and ordained men throughout all the world to proclaim that a godless and lawless heresy had sprung from one Jesus, a Galilean deceiver, whom we crucified, but his disciples stole him by night from the tomb, where he was laid when unfastened from the cross and now deceive men by asserting that he was risen from the dead and ascended to heaven."

Jewish tradition includes a book called the Toledoth Jesu that was written around AD 500. It's a story of Jesus' life that is different from the Bible. Most Jewish scholars don't think this book can be trusted as history. However, scholars do think its claim that Jesus' body was stolen is what Jews believed at that time. It also means they believed the tomb was empty.

"On the first day of the week his vold followers came to Queen Helene with the report that he who was slain was truly the Messiah and that he was not in his grave, he had ascended to heaven as he prophesied. Diligent search was made and he was not found in the grave where he had been buried."

Non-biblical evidence

Jewish tradition

Historical sources for the empty tomb

Toledoth Jesu

Friends and Enemies

APOSTLES

FRIENDS of Jesus who believe they saw him AFTER his death

APPEARANCES TO
THE DISCIPLES
  Mt 28:16-20
  Mk 16:14-18
  Lk 24:36-49
  Jn 20:19-23
  Jn 20:26-29
     (doubting Thomas)
  Jn 21:1-24
       (Sea of Galilee)
  Acts 1:1-11
  1 Cor 15:5, 7

Followers who believed
they saw Jesus:

Women at the tomb
Mt 28:9-10

Mary Magdalene:
Jn 20:14-17

Road to Emmaus:
Lk 24:13-32

Lk 24:33-49

Other followers were present
at the first appearance to the
apostles

1 Corinthians 15:6
"Then He appeared to over 500
brothers at one time; most of
them are still alive, but some
have fallen asleep."

the crowds are probably a mix of
apostles and followers of Jesus

Friends and *continued* Enemies

PAUL
SAUL OF TARSUS

ENEMY
PERSECUTED CHRISTIANS
(ACTS 8:1-3, 9:1-2)

TURNED FRIEND
ON THE ROAD TO DAMASCUS
TO PERSECUTE THE CHRISTIANS
THERE, PAUL BELIEVED HE
ENCOUNTERED JESUS.
(ACTS 9:3-19)

PREACHED THE GOSPEL ON MISSIONARY
JOURNEYS FOR THE NEXT 30 YEARS.
MARTYRED IN ROME
AROUND AD 64-65.

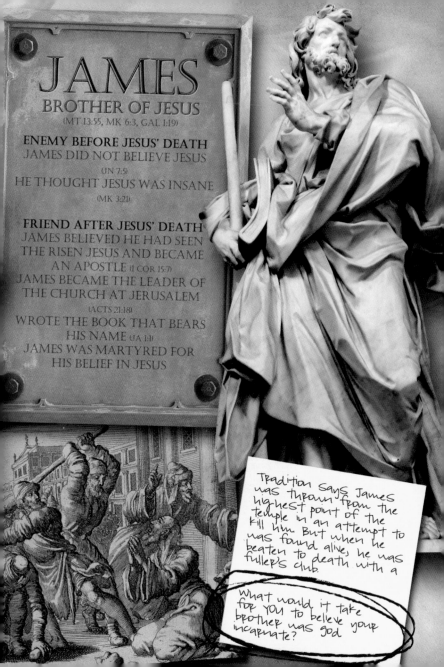

JAMES
BROTHER OF JESUS
(MT 13:55, MK 6:3, GAL 1:19)

ENEMY BEFORE JESUS' DEATH
JAMES DID NOT BELIEVE JESUS
(JN 7:5)
HE THOUGHT JESUS WAS INSANE
(MK 3:21)

FRIEND AFTER JESUS' DEATH
JAMES BELIEVED HE HAD SEEN
THE RISEN JESUS AND BECAME
AN APOSTLE (I COR 15:7)
JAMES BECAME THE LEADER OF
THE CHURCH AT JERUSALEM
(ACTS 21:18)
WROTE THE BOOK THAT BEARS
HIS NAME (JA 1:1)
JAMES WAS MARTYRED FOR
HIS BELIEF IN JESUS

Tradition says James was thrown from the highest point of the temple in an attempt to kill him. But when he was found alive, he was beaten to death with a fuller's club.

What would it take for you to believe your brother was God incarnate?

Alternate Theory:

Swoon

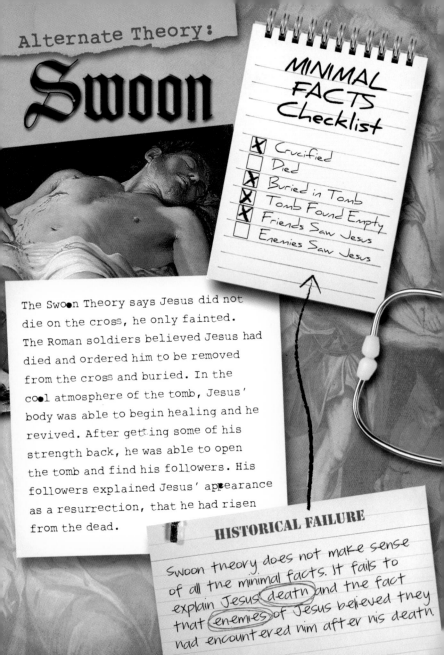

MINIMAL FACTS Checklist

- [x] Crucified
- [ ] Died
- [x] Buried in Tomb
- [x] Tomb Found Empty
- [x] Friends Saw Jesus
- [ ] Enemies Saw Jesus

The Swoon Theory says Jesus did not die on the cross, he only fainted. The Roman soldiers believed Jesus had died and ordered him to be removed from the cross and buried. In the cool atmosphere of the tomb, Jesus' body was able to begin healing and he revived. After getting some of his strength back, he was able to open the tomb and find his followers. His followers explained Jesus' appearance as a resurrection, that he had risen from the dead.

HISTORICAL FAILURE

Swoon theory does not make sense of all the minimal facts. It fails to explain Jesus death and the fact that enemies of Jesus believed they had encountered him after his death.

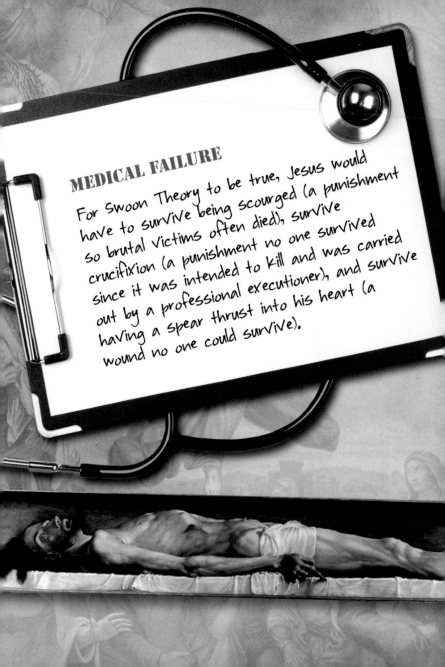

MEDICAL FAILURE

For Swoon Theory to be true, Jesus would have to survive being scourged (a punishment so brutal victims often died), survive crucifixion (a punishment no one survived since it was intended to kill and was carried out by a professional executioner), and survive having a spear thrust into his heart (a wound no one could survive).

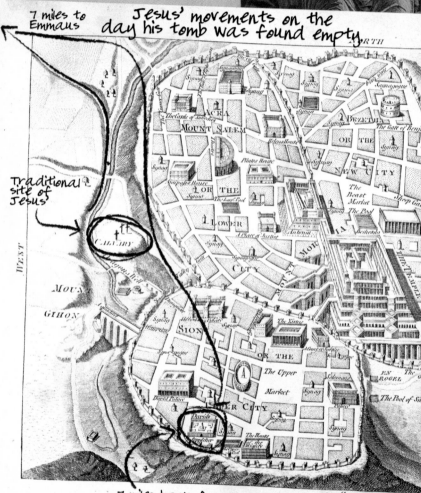

7 miles to Emmaus

Jesus' movements on the day his tomb was found empty

NORTH

Traditional site of Jesus

CALVARY

7 miles back from Emmaus plus the distance through Jerusalem to the upper Room.

BELIEVABILITY FAILURE

Even if the swoon theory could explain all the minimal facts, and even if Jesus could have survived the crucifixion, there is still a huge problem with the theory: it's just not believable. The whole point of the swoon theory is to explain what happened to Jesus without having to say a miracle happened. But the way it tries to explain what happened makes no sense.

If the swoon theory was true then after Jesus woke up in the tomb he would have had to pop his shoulders (and maybe his elbows) back into place, stand up on feet whose ankles were now probably useless, use his hands (also almost useless) to roll back a tombstone that weighed several hundred pounds, overpower the armed Roman soldiers guarding his tomb, walk seven miles to Emmaus, walk seven miles back to Jerusalem, walk through Jerusalem without being recognized or even calling attention to himself while wearing only his burial cloths and with strips of skin hanging from his body from the scourging, find where the disciples were hiding, find a way to break into the locked room without anyone seeing him enter, and then appear to them as if he was raised from the dead and that all was well! At the very least, the disciples would have thought he needed serious medical attention, not that he conquered death. For them to believe such a story would be a miracle!

Alternate Theory:

Wrong Tomb

MINIMAL FACTS Checklist

- ☒ Crucified
- ☒ Died
- ☒ Buried in Tomb
- ☒ Tomb Found Empty
- ☐ Friends Saw Jesus
- ☐ Enemies Saw Jesus

The Wrong Tomb theory says the reason why Jesus' followers found the tomb empty is that everyone simply went to the wrong tomb. After all, the tombs do look alike and it would be easy to confuse one with another. Since the tomb they mistook for Jesus' tomb was not being used, they explained it by claiming he had been resurrected from the dead

HISTORICAL FAILURE

The explanation of the Wrong Tomb does not make sense of the minimal facts. It doesn't give any reasons for why Jesus' followers said they saw him after he had been raised from the dead. And it fails to show why some of Jesus' enemies also claim to have seen Jesus after he had been killed and buried.

BELIEVABILITY FAILURE

By trying to explain why Jesus' followers thought they found the tomb empty, the Wrong Tomb theory ends up creating more problems than it solves. The women who discovered the tomb empty had seen Jesus buried and so they knew which tomb to look for. Not only that, but after telling the disciples what they found, they returned to the wrong tomb again. For a place that was so important to them, the idea that they went to the wrong tomb is very unlikely. When Peter and John were told by the women that the tomb was empty they ran ahead to see for themselves. This means they knew where to go, and yet when they got there they found the same thing—the tomb was empty. Did they go to the wrong tomb as well? And although many tombs may have looked alike, it would be hard to miss Jesus' tomb since it would have been the only one with Roman soldiers guarding it (some critics do not believe the tomb was guarded, though scripture teaches this in Mt 27:65).

This brings up the biggest problem of all: if Jesus' followers went to the wrong tomb, that means his body was still inside the right tomb. And if the Jewish leaders and/or the Romans wanted to stop Christianity and disprove it, all they had to do was open the right tomb to show that Jesus' body was still there. But they didn't because they couldn't.

Alternate Theory:

Wrong Tomb
Continued

Two kokhim in the Church of the Holy Sepulchre.

THE CHURCH OF THE HOLY SEPULCHRE WAS BUILT ON TOP OF AN OLD ROCK QUARRY, PART OF WHICH HAD BEEN TURNED INTO A GARDEN AFTER IT WAS NO LONGER USEFUL. THE QUARRY WAS ALSO USED TO BURY PEOPLE. TOMBS HAVE BEEN FOUND IN AT LEAST FOUR PLACES WITHIN THE CURRENT CHURCH WALLS. AND TWO DIFFERENT KINDS OF TOMBS HAVE BEEN FOUND. SOME OF THE TOMBS ARE CALLED KOKHIM AND ARE NICHES CUT INTO THE ROCK SO THAT THE BODY WAS PLACED PERPENDICULAR TO THE WALL. SEVERAL KOKHIM WERE OFTEN CUT INTO THE WALLS OF A SINGLE ROOM SO THAT MANY PEOPLE COULD BE BURIED AT ONCE. A STONE WAS THEN ROLLED IN FRONT OF THE ENTRANCE TO THE ROOM. A SECOND KIND OF TOMB FOUND IN THE CHURCH WAS A MORE EXPENSIVE AND LESS COMMON TOMB CALLED AN ARCOSOLIUM. IT HAD A SMALL ENTRY ROOM (CLOSED BY A ROLLING STONE) AND AN INNER ROOM THAT HAD BENCHES OR NICHES CUT PARALLEL TO THE WALLS. THE ROOM MAY HAVE A BENCH PER WALL. THIS SECOND KIND OF TOMB IS WHAT THE TRADITIONAL TOMB OF JESUS IS. IF THAT'S TRUE THEN THE IDEA THAT JESUS' FOLLOWERS WENT TO THE WRONG TOMB IS EVEN MORE UNLIKELY SINCE THERE WERE PROBABLY NOT VERY MANY ACROSOLIA TO CHOOSE FROM. AND IF IT WAS A KOKH TOMB THEN THEY COULDN'T HAVE GONE TO JUST ANY TOMB, SINCE THEY WERE LOOKING FOR A PARTICULAR KIND. AND SINCE DIFFERENT ROOMS HAD DIFFERENT NUMBERS AND CONFIGURATIONS OF KOKHIM, THE CHANCE OF CONFUSING TOMBS WOULD BE VERY SMALL.

The burial bench inside the traditional tomb of Jesus (top) and an acrosolium found in Germany (bottom).

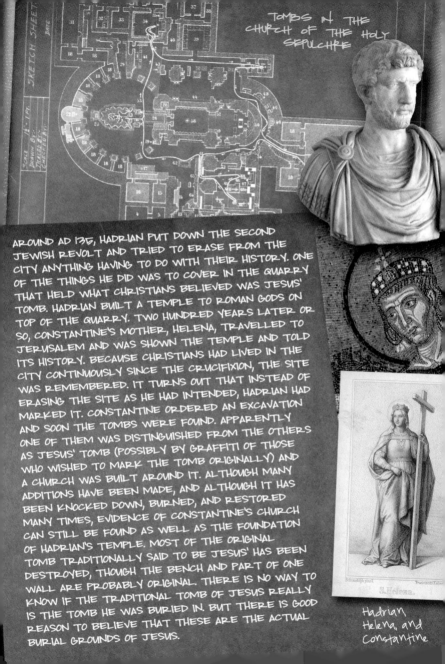

AROUND AD 135, HADRIAN PUT DOWN THE SECOND JEWISH REVOLT AND TRIED TO ERASE FROM THE CITY ANYTHING HAVING TO DO WITH THEIR HISTORY. ONE OF THE THINGS HE DID WAS TO COVER IN THE QUARRY THAT HELD WHAT CHRISTIANS BELIEVED WAS JESUS' TOMB. HADRIAN BUILT A TEMPLE TO ROMAN GODS ON TOP OF THE QUARRY. TWO HUNDRED YEARS LATER OR SO, CONSTANTINE'S MOTHER, HELENA, TRAVELLED TO JERUSALEM AND WAS SHOWN THE TEMPLE AND TOLD ITS HISTORY. BECAUSE CHRISTIANS HAD LIVED IN THE CITY CONTINUOUSLY SINCE THE CRUCIFIXION, THE SITE WAS REMEMBERED. IT TURNS OUT THAT INSTEAD OF ERASING THE SITE AS HE HAD INTENDED, HADRIAN HAD MARKED IT. CONSTANTINE ORDERED AN EXCAVATION AND SOON THE TOMBS WERE FOUND. APPARENTLY ONE OF THEM WAS DISTINGUISHED FROM THE OTHERS AS JESUS' TOMB (POSSIBLY BY GRAFFITI OF THOSE WHO WISHED TO MARK THE TOMB ORIGINALLY) AND A CHURCH WAS BUILT AROUND IT. ALTHOUGH MANY ADDITIONS HAVE BEEN MADE, AND ALTHOUGH IT HAS BEEN KNOCKED DOWN, BURNED, AND RESTORED MANY TIMES, EVIDENCE OF CONSTANTINE'S CHURCH CAN STILL BE FOUND AS WELL AS THE FOUNDATION OF HADRIAN'S TEMPLE. MOST OF THE ORIGINAL TOMB TRADITIONALLY SAID TO BE JESUS' HAS BEEN DESTROYED, THOUGH THE BENCH AND PART OF ONE WALL ARE PROBABLY ORIGINAL. THERE IS NO WAY TO KNOW IF THE TRADITIONAL TOMB OF JESUS REALLY IS THE TOMB HE WAS BURIED IN. BUT THERE IS GOOD REASON TO BELIEVE THAT THESE ARE THE ACTUAL BURIAL GROUNDS OF JESUS.

Hadrian, Helena, and Constantine

Alternate Theory:

Stolen Body

MINIMAL FACTS Checklist

- ☒ Crucified
- ☒ Died
- ☒ Buried in Tomb
- ☒ Tomb Found Empty
- ☐ Friends Saw Jesus
- ☐ Enemies Saw Jesus

The stolen body theory says someone broke into Jesus' tomb and took the body. There are only three groups who might have a reason to steal the body: The Romans, the Jews, and Jesus' disciples.

HISTORICAL FAILURE

Saying that Jesus' body was stolen does not make sense of the minimal facts. If the Romans or Jews stole the body it doesn't give any reasons for why Jesus' followers said they saw him after he had been raised from the dead. And no matter who stole the body, it fails to show why some of Jesus' enemies also claim to have seen Jesus after he had been killed and buried.

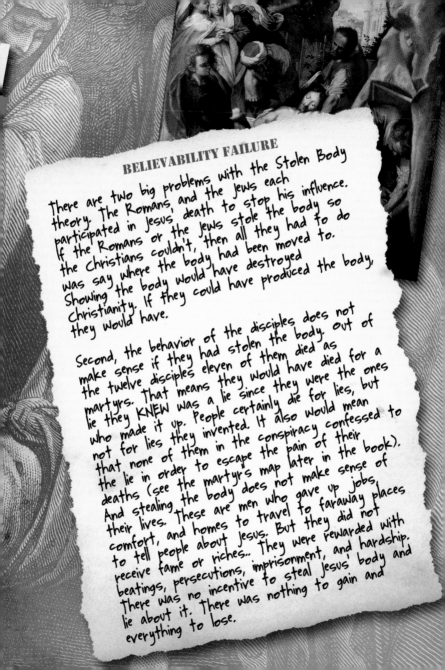

BELIEVABILITY FAILURE

There are two big problems with the Stolen Body theory. The Romans, and the Jews each participated in Jesus' death to stop his influence. If the Romans or the Jews stole the body so the Christians couldn't, then all they had to do was say where the body had been moved to. Showing the body would have destroyed Christianity. If they could have produced the body, they would have.

Second, the behavior of the disciples does not make sense if they had stolen the body. Out of the twelve disciples eleven of them died as martyrs. That means they would have died for a lie they KNEW was a lie since they were the ones who made it up. People certainly die for lies, but not for lies they invented. It also would mean that none of them in the conspiracy confessed to the lie in order to escape the pain of their deaths (see the martyr's map later in the book). And stealing the body does not make sense of their lives. These are men who gave up jobs, comfort, and homes to travel to faraway places to tell people about Jesus. But they did not receive fame or riches... they were rewarded with beatings, persecutions, imprisonment, and hardship. There was no incentive to steal Jesus' body and lie about it. There was nothing to gain and everything to lose.

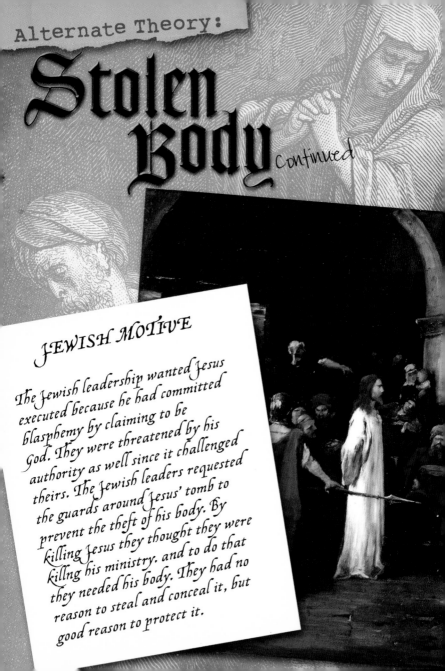

Stolen Body *Continued*

JEWISH MOTIVE

The Jewish leadership wanted Jesus executed because he had committed blasphemy by claiming to be God. They were threatened by his authority as well since it challenged theirs. The Jewish leaders requested the guards around Jesus' tomb to prevent the theft of his body. By killing Jesus they thought they were killing his ministry, and to do that they needed his body. They had no reason to steal and conceal it, but good reason to protect it.

HISTORICAL ADVANTAGE

Of all the alternative theories, the Stolen Body is the only explanation that dates back to the first century. This makes it more historically important than the other theories since it uses the same evidence from the same time period and tries to explain the events in the same historical and cultural setting.

One of the interesting things about having another first century explanation is that it backs up several important points that many of the other theories can't explain. The most significant of these is that the tomb was empty. The empty tomb might be the hardest minimal fact to explain away.

ROMAN MOTIVE

THE ROMANS EXECUTED JESUS TO PREVENT UNREST AMONG THE JEWS, A PEOPLE ROME HAD DIFFICULTY RULING. ALSO, GOVERNOR PONTIUS PILATE WAS TOLD THAT JESUS CLAIMED TO BE A KING AND THEREFORE WAS A THREAT TO ROME. ROME'S MOTIVE IN KILLING JESUS WAS TO STOP HIS MOVEMENT. THEY HAD NO REASON TO STEAL HIS BODY UNLESS THEY PLANNED TO BE ABLE TO SHOW IT TO MAKE SURE THE JESUS MOVEMENT WAS NO LONGER A THREAT. A DEAD BODY EQUALS A DEAD MOVEMENT.

DEATHS OF THE DISCIPLES

Peter - Crucified, Rome

James - sword, Jerusalem

James Alphaeus - stoned, Jerusalem

Matthew - Beheaded, Nadabah, Ethiopia

Bartholomew - Beaten, crucified, flayed,
   beheaded, Albinopolis, Armenia

Thomas - speared, India

Simon the Zealot - crucified, Britain

Matthias - stoned, beheaded, Jerusalem

Philip - crucified, Hieropolis

Andrew - crucified, Edessa, Greece

Jude - crucified, Edessa, Mesopotamia

DEATHS OF THE EVANGELISTS

Mark - dragged through the streets,
   Alexandria

Luke - crucified, Ephesus (though some
   tradition says he died naturally)

Some of these men have other traditions giving a different story of how and where they were martyred, but none of them have traditions that claim they escaped martyrdom (with the possible exception of Luke).

The reason the behavior of the disciples is important is because no alternate theory can explain why the disciples acted the way they did. Why would they invent the story of the resurrection and then spend the rest of their lives travelling the world spreading a lie if what they got in return was hardship, torture, and death? It didn't bring them wealth or comfort or any other advantage. Not only that, not a single person in the conspiracy confessed to the lie, even though they had plenty of opportunity to tell the truth as they were being tortured and, in many cases, slowly executed. That is the behavior of people who believe they are telling the truth.

BRITAIN

Mare Germanicum

Martyr's Map

INDIA

ETHIOPIA

EDESSA

MOESIA
SUPERIOR

MOESIA
INFERIOR

Pontus Euxinus

THRACIA

MACEDONIA

BITHYNIA ET PONTUS

CAPPADOCIA

EPIRUS

EDESSA

GALATIA

ATHENS

EPHESUS

HIEROPOLIS

LYCIA

CILICIA

SYRIA

PAMPHYLIA

CYPRUS

Mare Internum

IUDAEA

JERUSALEM

CYRENAICA

ARABIA

ALEXANDRIA

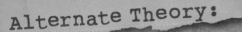

Alternate Theory:

Legend
version 1: conspiracy

There are two versions of the theory that says the Resurrection is a legend. According to one version of the legend theory, Jesus' disciples wanted to keep his teaching alive after his death. To do this they invented stories of his bodily resurrection and appearances to give a framework for preserving his teaching and draw attention to them.

MINIMAL FACTS Checklist

- [x] Crucified
- [x] Died
- [x] Buried in Tomb
- [ ] Tomb Found Empty
- [ ] Friends Saw Jesus
- [ ] Enemies Saw Jesus

HISTORICAL FAILURE

This version of the legend theory fails to explain three of the minimal facts.

It does not account for the fact that the tomb was found empty.

And it doesn't make sense of why both friends of Jesus and some enemies of Jesus believed they saw him after his death and burial

BELIEVABILITY FAILURE 1

At the time of Jesus' death, the culture treated women so poorly that they were not seen as being trustworthy enough to testify in court.

If the disciples were trying to invent a story people would actually believe, why would they have the tomb discovered by the women (who would not be believed) instead of by important, male disciples that would be authoritative like Peter, James, or John?

First century Roman/Jewish historian Josephus records in his book *Antiquities of the Jews* (IV.xiii) that the testimony of women was not to be believed in a court of law.

"Put not trust in a single witness. Let there be three or at least two whose evidence shall be accredited by their past lives. From women let no evidence be accepted because of the levity and temerity of their sex."

Alternate Theory:

Legend

version 1: conspiracy

Continued

BELIEVABILITY FAILURE 2

If the disciples created the story of the resurrection, then what happened to the body? If the body was still in the tomb, all the Romans or Jews needed to do to kill christianity was open the tomb and show that the body was not resurrected. But they did not. In fact, the first century evidence shows the Jews believed the tomb was empty and the body was stolen. But the stolen body theory fails to account for all the facts. And neither the stolen body nor the legend theory can explain why the disciples would give up everything to spend their lives spreading a lie and dying horrible deaths (except for John, who died of old age).

POST CARD

BELIEVABILITY FAILURE 3

If the disciples wanted to make up a story about Jesus' resurrection, then why did they include details that could be investigated and proven false? Wouldn't it be better for them to make claims that were vague or could be interpreted many ways? And why would the disciples then proclaim these made-up facts in the very city where the events occurred and could be checked-out? Why didn't they do it in Galilee or somewhere where the story would make it difficult to look into? It doesn't make sense.

Alternate Theory:

Legend
version 2: development

The other version of the legend theory says that in the years after Jesus' death stories about him developed and evolved. Over time these stories started to claim Jesus had supernatural powers and include miraculous events, the biggest of which was his resurrection. No one was trying to lie about Jesus' life, they were just trying to honor him. But these traditions were passed down as history and we need to distinguish the Jesus of history from the Christ of the Bible.

HISTORICAL FAILURE

The development version of the legend theory fails to explain the same three minimal facts as the other legend theory for many of the same reasons.

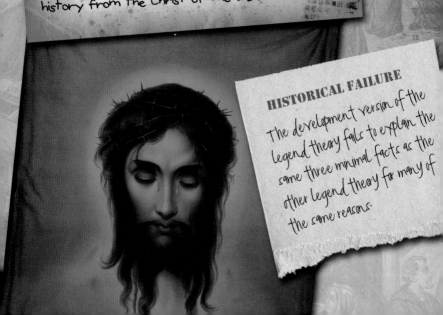

2 r.k.

The Legend Theory doesn't make sense of the behavior of the disciples.

1

The Legend Theory doesn't make sense of why the women are credited with discovering the empty tomb.

The Legend Theory would have developed when apostles were still alive and they would have corrected the false stories.

The Legend Theory doesn't make sense of resurrection being proclaimed in Jerusalem.

13

Legend

version 2: *Continued* development

Development or Complement?

MARK 15:46–47

After he bought some fine linen, he took Him down and wrapped Him in the linen. Then he placed Him in a tomb cut out of the rock, and rolled a stone against the entrance to the tomb. Now Mary Magdalene and Mary the mother of Joses were watching where He was placed.

MATTHEW 27:59–61

So Joseph took the body, wrapped it in clean, fine linen, and placed it in his new tomb, which he had cut into the rock. He left after rolling a great stone against the entrance of the tomb. Mary Magdalene and the other Mary were seated there, facing the tomb.

Some scholars claim to see the development of legend when the gospels are placed in the order they were probably written. For example, Mark calls the burial shroud "linen," Matthew adds it was "clean, fine linen," Luke calls it "fine linen," and John adds the linen was wrapped in "aromatic spices". But do these differences really show a legend developing or simply complementary descriptions of the same thing, to which each author added a bit of information?

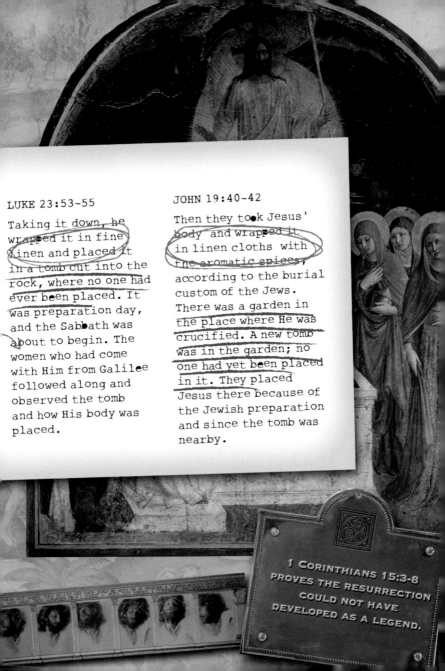

LUKE 23:53-55

Taking it down, he wrapped it in fine linen and placed it in a tomb cut into the rock, where no one had ever been placed. It was preparation day, and the Sabbath was about to begin. The women who had come with Him from Galilee followed along and observed the tomb and how His body was placed.

JOHN 19:40-42

Then they took Jesus' body and wrapped it in linen cloths with the aromatic spices, according to the burial custom of the Jews. There was a garden in the place where He was crucified. A new tomb was in the garden; no one had yet been placed in it. They placed Jesus there because of the Jewish preparation and since the tomb was nearby.

1 CORINTHIANS 15:3-8 PROVES THE RESURRECTION COULD NOT HAVE DEVELOPED AS A LEGEND.

Oldest Creed

1 Corinthians 15:3-7

Ruins of Corinth

Counting backwards 14 years from the famine relief visit gives us the date of Paul's conversion. In the first century time was sometimes calculated inclusively, meaning the 14 years could be counted by thinking of the starting year as 1 instead of 0. That's why his conversion is given a range of years.

1 Cor 15:3-7
31-4
Creed existed prior to Paul's conversion

Jerusalem Council
48 (Acts 15:22)
Preceded 2nd missionary journey

Famine Relief Visit
45-7 (Acts 11:27-30)
Dated by first century Jewish/Roman historian Josephus, who mentions the famine in Antiquites of the Jews, 20.2.5.

Conversion
32-5 (Gal. 2:1)
Went to Jerusalem a second time 14 years after conversion.

30 or 33
Crucifixion

TIMELINE OF PAUL

To prove that the story of Jesus' resurrection did not develop as a legend we would have to know what the very earliest followers of Jesus believed about him and about what happened to him a couple of days after his death. The problem is that the writings of the New Testament were written between about 20 and 60 years after the crucifixion, a length of time some critics say could allow a legend to be born. If we had some writing from the time immediately following the death of Jesus we could see if his resurrection and its meaning were a part of what his disciples believed. Fortunately, we DO have a writing from those earliest days of Christianity.

Before the New Testament was completed, part of how Christians remembered the teachings of the faith was by using creeds, which are short summaries of beliefs that could be easily memorized, and by using hymns. Many creeds and hymns are included in the writings of the New Testament, which vouches for their accuracy. And at least some of them predate even the earliest New Testament scripture. 1 Corinthians 15:3-7 is one of those creeds.

Gallio proconsul of Achaia
51-2 (Acts 18:12)

Dated by the Gallio or Delphi inscription

1 Corinthians 15:3-7 is probably the oldest part of the New Testament.

c. 64-67
Death

Oldest Creed
Continued

1 Corinthians 15:3-7

Paul implies the passage is a creed and that it existed before his conversion. This is the teaching he himself was given when he became a believer.

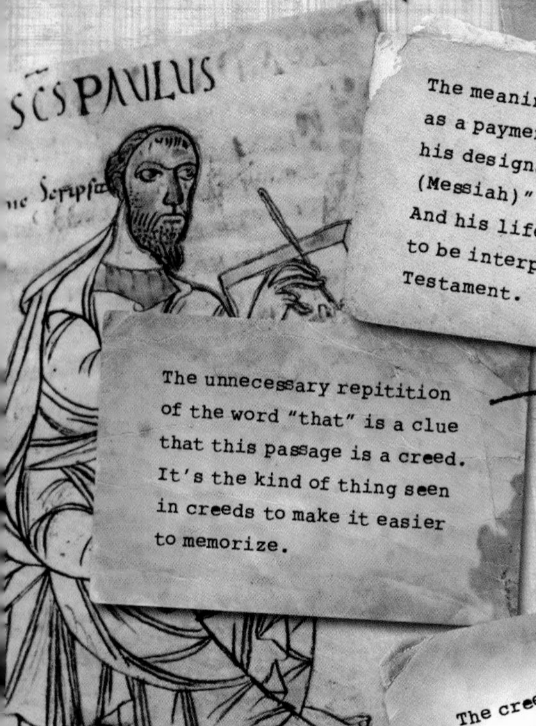

The meaning of Jesus' death as a payment for sin and his designation as "Christ (Messiah)" did not develop. And his life and death were to be interpreted by the Old Testament.

SCS PAULUS

ne Scriptu

The unnecessary repitition of the word "that" is a clue that this passage is a creed. It's the kind of thing seen in creeds to make it easier to memorize.

The creed includes a list of witnesses to Jesus' resurrection appearances, which means these witnesses could be asked about what they saw and what they believed it meant.

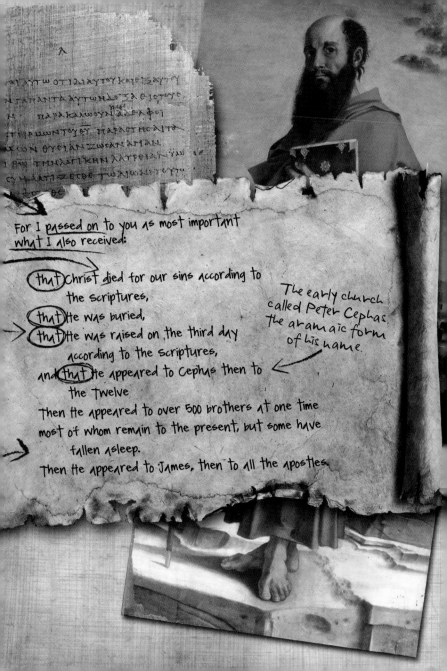

For I passed on to you as most important
what I also received:

that Christ died for our sins according to
the scriptures,

that He was buried,

that He was raised on the third day
according to the scriptures,

and that He appeared to Cephas then to
the Twelve

Then He appeared to over 500 brothers at one time
most of whom remain to the present, but some have
fallen asleep.

Then He appeared to James, then to all the apostles.

The early church
called Peter Cephas,
the aramaic form
of his name.

Hallucination

The Hallucination theory says that the followers of Jesus were so upset by his death that they began to think they saw him even though he wasn't there. Some had private hallucinations, others had group hallucinations, and sometimes there were mass hallucinations where several hundred people all believed they saw Jesus.

MINIMAL FACTS Checklist

- [x] Crucified
- [x] Died
- [x] Buried in Tomb
- [ ] Tomb Found Empty
- [ ] Friends Saw Jesus
- [ ] Enemies Saw Jesus

HISTORICAL FAILURE

Only three of the six facts that need to be explained are covered by claiming everyone who thought they saw Jesus after his death was hallucinating.

Hallucinations are like dreams people have when they're awake. But no matter how vivid someone's dream or hallucination is, they would never confuse the experience with reality so much that they would die for it. Just as people are easily convinced their dream was not reality, people can be talked out of believing a hallucination is real.

Hallucination Continued

BELIEVABILITY FAILURE

Whether in Jerusalem, or on the roads outside Jerusalem, or on a boat in Galilee, several hundred people (many who knew Jesus before his death) all said they saw him and received information from him. Although some people were alone with him and others were in groups or crowds, the different reports give a unified picture of Jesus and don't contradict each other. The people who believed they encountered a risen Jesus not only spoke as if it really happened, but their descriptions of what Jesus said and how he acted all agreed as if they'd seen the same thing. People may hallucinate at the same time, but each person's hallucination is different since each person is only seeing someting in their own mind, not in the real world. There is no way for hallucinations to give the same information since each hallucination is unique to the person having it. Hallucinations are clearly not the kind of thing being reported here.

Fishermen on the Sea of Galilee

Jerusalem Street

Road to Jerusalem

PERSISTENT PROBLEM

If the Hallucination theory is true then the body is still in the tomb. Once again the empty tomb is a problem for a theory that denies the Resurrection.

Alternate Theory:

Twin
a.k.a Substitution

The Twin or Substitution theory says Jesus had a twin brother who switched places with him and died in Jesus' place. Two days later Jesus came out of hiding claiming that he had been resurrected from the dead.

MINIMAL FACTS Checklist

- [x] Crucified
- [x] Died
- [x] Buried in Tomb
- [ ] Tomb Found Empty
- [x] Friends Saw Jesus
- [x] Enemies Saw Jesus

BELIEVABILITY FAILURE 1

For the Twin / Substitution theory to work, Jesus' twin would have had to follow Jesus around without being recognized and be willing to swap places with him just before being arrested so he could willingly die in Jesus' place in order that Jesus could create the hoax of being resurrected from the dead. Who would willingly die for a hoax their brother wanted to play? Also, this deception goes against everything we know about Jesus' character and teaching.

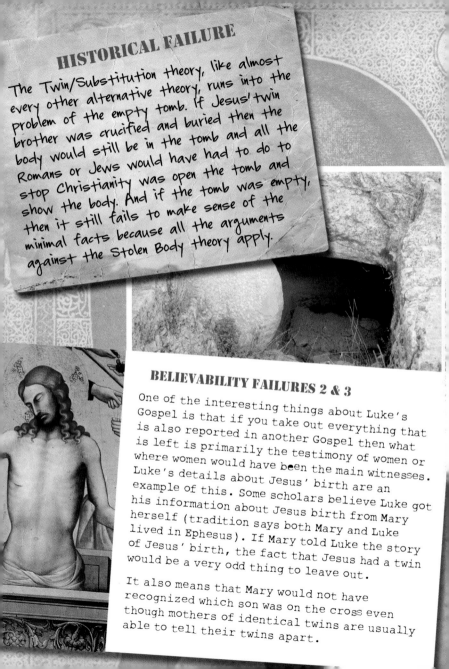

HISTORICAL FAILURE

The Twin/Substitution theory, like almost every other alternative theory, runs into the problem of the empty tomb. If Jesus' twin brother was crucified and buried then the body would still be in the tomb and all the Romans or Jews would have had to do to stop Christianity was open the tomb and show the body. And if the tomb was empty, then it still fails to make sense of the minimal facts because all the arguments against the Stolen Body theory apply.

BELIEVABILITY FAILURES 2 & 3

One of the interesting things about Luke's Gospel is that if you take out everything that is also reported in another Gospel then what is left is primarily the testimony of women or where women would have been the main witnesses. Luke's details about Jesus' birth are an example of this. Some scholars believe Luke got his information about Jesus birth from Mary herself (tradition says both Mary and Luke lived in Ephesus). If Mary told Luke the story of Jesus' birth, the fact that Jesus had a twin would be a very odd thing to leave out.

It also means that Mary would not have recognized which son was on the cross even though mothers of identical twins are usually able to tell their twins apart.

Twin
a.k.a Substitution
Islamic versions

Islam's holy book, the Qur'an, gives a combination of the Twin/Substitution and Hallucination theories in Surah 4:157-158. As a result, it cannot account for the empty tomb, the friends that believed they saw Jesus, and the enemies who believed they saw Jesus.

In addition, the Qur'an was written about 600 years or so after Jesus died. This doesn't necessarily mean what it says about Jesus is false, but at face value it would be less trustworthy than the New Testament accounts and early Jewish tradition, both of which are from the first century and contradict the Qur'an in different ways.

And for saying, "We killed (the Messiah) Jesus, son of Mary," the messenger of GOD. They never killed him, they never crucified him – they were made to think that they did. All factions are full of doubt concerning this issue. They possess no knowledge; they only conjecture. For certain, they never killed him.

Instead GOD raised him to Him; GOD is Almighty, Most Wise.

(Authorized English Version)

Although the Gospel of Barnabas is attributed to Paul's partner in evangelism, it was probably written in the middle ages. In chapters 216-219 it tells how Judas was so filled with regret at betraying Jesus that he went to visit Jesus in his prison cell. There God transformed Judas to look and sound like Jesus, and as a result Judas took Jesus' place on the cross while God took Jesus directly to Heaven.

This account combines elements of the Twin/Substitution, Hallucination, and Stolen Body theories and therefore fails to make sense of the minimal facts.

216. Judas entered impetuously before all into the chamber whence Jesus had been taken up. Whereupon the wonderful God acted wonderfully, insomuch that Judas was so changed in speech and in face to be like Jesus that we believed him to be Jesus...the soldiery entered, and laid their hands upon Judas, because he was in every way like to Jesus.

217. ...Truly I say that the voice, the face, and the person of Judas were so like to Jesus, that his disciples and believers entirely believed that he was Jesus...they obtained from the governor the body of Judas to bury it...

218. Those disciples who did not fear God went by night [and] stole the body of Judas and hid it, spreading a report that Jesus was risen again.

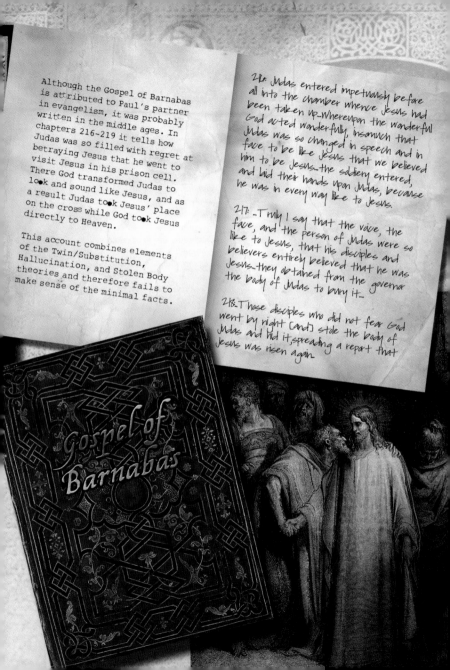

Resurrection

The only explanation to make sense of all the minimal facts—the facts that even the most skeptical scholars agree with—is the explanation found in the New Testament. The confidence Paul has in the historical, bodily resurrection of Jesus is backed up by the evidence. That's his point in 1 Corinthians 15:12-19. And that's why we can have the same kind of confidence—a confidence we can bet our lives on.

He Himself

bore our sins

in His body on

the tree, so

that, having

died to sins, we

might live for

righteousness;

by His wounding

you have been

healed.

———————

1 Peter 2:24

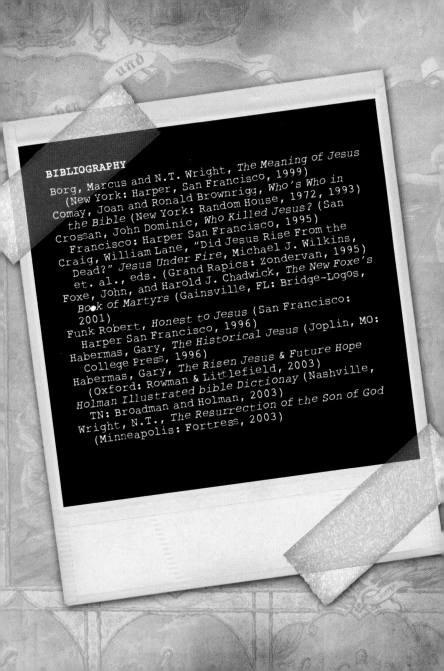

BIBLIOGRAPHY

Borg, Marcus and N.T. Wright, *The Meaning of Jesus* (New York: Harper, San Francisco, 1999)

Comay, Joan and Ronald Brownrigg, *Who's Who in the Bible* (New York: Random House, 1972, 1993)

Crossan, John Dominic, *Who Killed Jesus?* (San Francisco: Harper San Francisco, 1995)

Craig, William Lane, "Did Jesus Rise From the Dead?" *Jesus Under Fire*, Michael J. Wilkins, et. al., eds. (Grand Rapics: Zondervan, 1995)

Foxe, John, and Harold J. Chadwick, *The New Foxe's Book of Martyrs* (Gainsville, FL: Bridge-Logos, 2001)

Funk Robert, *Honest to Jesus* (San Francisco: Harper San Francisco, 1996)

Habermas, Gary, *The Historical Jesus* (Joplin, MO: College Press, 1996)

Habermas, Gary, *The Risen Jesus & Future Hope* (Oxford: Rowman & Littlefield, 2003)

Holman Illustrated bible Dictionay (Nashville, TN: Broadman and Holman, 2003)

Wright, N.T., *The Resurrection of the Son of God* (Minneapolis: Fortress, 2003)

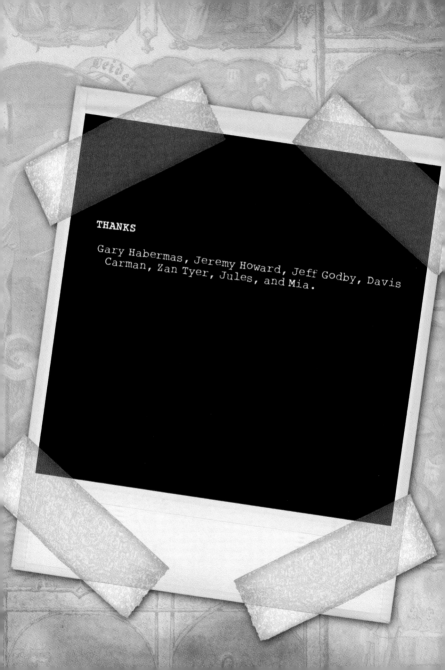

THANKS

Gary Habermas, Jeremy Howard, Jeff Godby, Davis Carman, Zan Tyer, Jules, and Mia.